The Rules of Office Politics

THE RULES
OF OFFICE
POLITICS

ROB YEUNG

CYAN

Copyright © 2006 Rob Yeung

First published in 2006 by:

Marshall Cavendish Limited
119 Wardour Street
London W1F 0UW
United Kingdom
T: +44 (0)20 7565 6000
F: +44 (0)20 7734 6221
E: sales@marshallcavendish.co.uk
Online bookstore: www.marshallcavendish.co.uk

and

Cyan Communications Limited
119 Wardour Street
London W1F 0UW
United Kingdom
T: +44 (0)20 7565 6120
E: sales@cyanbooks.com
www.cyanbooks.com

The right of Rob Yeung to be identified as the author of this work has been asserted
by him in accordance with the Copyright, Designs and Patents Act 1988.

A CIP record for this book is available from the British Library

ISBN-13 978-1-904879-85-5
ISBN-10 1-904879-85-3

Printed and bound in Great Britain
by TJ International Ltd, Padstow, Cornwall

Contents

Foreword

Working life ain't simple any more. There was a time when you worked hard, you got looked after by your employer, and you just carried on until you received your gold carriage clock on retirement. But that simple career path is dead. There are more threats in the world – mergers and acquisitions, globalization and jobs being outsourced or offshored, downsizing programs and job cuts. And these have turned the workplace into a minefield of treacherous personalities, unexploded resentments and ticking egos. Who can you really trust? What do you need to do or say to get ahead?

The good news is there are more opportunities too. You aren't tied to the one employer any more – you can move around and seek bigger pay rises, greater responsibility, more interesting challenges. Employers no longer look down on people who want to take career breaks to go traveling or do something different. You can go freelance or set up your own business and try to make your first million. The world is your oyster.

In this complex world of work, the rules of work have changed. We can all think of people who got promoted who didn't deserve to be. Come to think of it, we can all probably think of someone who does deserve to get promoted, but hasn't been. To add insult to injury, on top of our day-to-day jobs, we're expected to deal with office politics, to be good leaders and team players, and to network. And how do you get headhunted exactly? All of these are things that no one ever really tells you how to do.

Well, this series tells you how to do these things. And this book delves into the rules of office politics – the game that is played but rarely talked about. Make no mistake: politicking is a game like any other – with rules to be learnt. Someone once quipped (a guy by the name of Leo Durocher, if you must know), "show me a good loser and I'll show you an idiot." Do you want to be a loser and an idiot?

No, thought not.

But you might be thinking that office politics involves skulking and scheming, colluding and conniving. And it's true that a lot of that goes on. But that doesn't mean that all politicking at work is automatically bad. Understanding the rules of politics can help you achieve outcomes that are beneficial for the organization and in an ethical fashion too. Or, if you insist on engaging in underhand politicking, then a better understanding of its rules will at least help you avoid getting caught. All in all, it's a skill that everyone needs to succeed at work.

But let's cut to the chase. After all, who has the time to sit and read hefty management tomes? Too often, an author has a handful of great ideas, but then ruins it by spending hundreds and hundreds of pages explaining it carefully in excruciating detail, giving too much background and yawn yawn yawn ... I've lost the will to live.

When I read one of those books, I start to flick through the pages with increasing impatience – wanting to shout, "Come On, Get To The Point!" So this book is short and full of practical, pithy advice.

If you have ever wanted to know how to get ahead in your career – but don't have the time to plow through bible-sized manuals or books that talk down to you – then this is the book for you. Feel free to flick through and find the chapters that are most interesting for you.

Finally, drop me an email if you would like to share any of your political horror stories or have tips you'd like to share. Honestly, it would be good to hear from you!

Rob Yeung
rob@talentspace.co.uk

INTRODUCTION

Backstabbing colleagues, scheming rivals, incompetent teammates, conniving types, self-serving spin doctors and toxic bosses. Welcome to Planet Politics.

Let's be honest about it. The modern workplace is a hotbed of office politics. Bad stuff can happen to good people, and much of it comes down to office politics. In fact, most professionals would positively love their jobs – if it weren't for certain people and the politics.

When I started to write this book, my colleagues and I here at Talentspace surveyed nearly 200 clients and other contacts to tell us about their experience of office politics. They came up with a (very long) list of words and phrases that included: lying, cheating, manipulating, schmoozing, and being two-faced. Not to mention maneuvering, rumor mongering, plotting, brown-nosing, and sucking up. Oh, and don't forget behaviors such as blatant self-promotion, scheming, and even using sex as a weapon at work.

Yes, all of these go on in the workplace. You can probably think of plenty of people who use such tactics to further their careers. But why do they do it? Because all workplaces are really about competition. Much of it is subtle and unspoken, but to some extent or other, nearly everyone is competing for budgets, resources, and opportunities to work on exciting projects. And then there's competition for promotions, time with important colleagues or customers, prestige, recognition, bigger salaries, and, of course, power. But the very fact that people do plot and scheme at work should illustrate one of the truths of politicking – that politics delivers results.

While we're at it, here's another uncomfortable truth – politicking happens whether you like it or not. Yes, some people try to be noble and refuse to play the political game; they focus on their jobs and work hard in the hopes of being noticed and rewarded for their efforts. But sadly there are limited opportunities in any organization and, more often than not, these sorts of people just end up being overlooked or ignored. Do you want to be overlooked or ignored?

Of course not.

You'd think that would be a silly question – whether anyone would choose to be overlooked or ignored. But too many people try in vain to get ahead without playing the game of office politics. If you think you can succeed without getting political, you need to wake up. Wake up and smell that coffee.

Many people refuse to play the political game, believing it to require underhand tactics and a malicious intent. But politics are not automatically bad. Politicking merely describes the act of scrutinizing relationships at work and learning how to influence others more effectively. It usually involves going through informal channels rather than officially sanctioned ones, but that doesn't make it bad in and of itself.

Politicking is not intrinsically good or bad – it is merely a tool. People can choose to use their understanding of politics to influence people and achieve goals that are good for the organization as well as themselves. Even in the most friendly and supportive of organizations, people don't always agree – so having an understanding of politics and how to exert influence can help you to pull people together and achieve outcomes that are in the organization's best interests too.

In fact, if you do try to manipulate and use people, you will probably get caught. You could be tarnished with the label of being "political," which can make people refuse to trust you or want to listen to you again. So effective politicking has to be as much about give as it is about take.

But "office politics" does have rather negative connotations. Personally, I choose to use the term "political savvy" to refer to the skill of reading and using relationships at work. And enhancing your political savvy is as simple as ABC:

- Assessing the political landscape. Too many would-be political players fall down because they try to get involved without properly understanding the currents and undercurrents within the organization. So observe, analyze, categorize and understand the dynamics and web of relationships that govern how people behave in order to succeed. Learn the rules before you play the game.

- Building significant relationships. The next step is to formulate a plan to build relationships with people who can help you achieve your goals. But it isn't merely about being nice to everyone, because the canny political player realizes that not all people at work are created equally. Learn to influence and build relationships with the right people.

- Confronting adversaries. People are usually the biggest obstacle to giving us what we want. Every now and then you may come across certain individuals who are more of an obstacle than most. Whether it is a colleague who is slightly bad-tempered or someone with downright malicious intentions, this step is about tackling the unsatisfactory relationships that prevent you from achieving your goals. Learn to neutralize threats to your career.

Political savvy is about getting what you want. It's a way of thinking about goals and how to achieve them through relationships. Even if you don't have power or influence to begin with, you can accrue it through observation, planning and execution. Whether you want to pursue your organization's goals or your own personal ones – well, that's up to you. But whatever you want, let's help you to achieve it.

ASSESSING THE POLITICAL LANDSCAPE

Once upon a time, a young management consultant got offered a new job. He had been working in a big consultancy with thousands of consultants and was asked to join a niche consultancy with just a dozen. The directors at the new company told him that they wanted him to shake them up with new ideas from the bigger firm. So he set about pointing out inefficiencies and suggesting better ways of working. But within weeks, he was told that he was being too bossy and interfering.

Unfortunately I was that young consultant. And I learned that, when it comes to trying to achieve results, you first need to shut up and observe the rules of the game. I was trying to play a game when I didn't understand the rules. Heck, I didn't even know the name of the game.

In retrospect, it all made sense. The directors had been running the company for years and were fairly pleased with how it was going. So when they said they wanted big ideas, they really wanted flattery about how successful they had been in growing their little business. What they actually wanted were small ideas, modest tweaks to how their business worked.

Nowadays I get to see a lot of successful people in action. And I've observed that successful people take the time to learn the rules. Successful people understand that the unspoken rules of politics are more important for getting ahead than given goals or explicit targets. When it comes to playing the political game, the first stage is to observe, analyze, categorize, and understand. Only when you discover the unspoken rules, the identities of the main players and their tactics, can you enter the fray.

Understand harsh realities

Life is tough. And organizational life is tougher. So let's get some ground rules sorted. Just as your parents were supposed to tell you about the facts of life, I'm going to share with you the four facts of organizational life.

Fact 1: Your organization does not care about you. The managers may say that they care about you. But then again, don't all organizations claim, "Our people are our greatest asset"?

The reality is that most organizations are focused on reaching their goals – which are usually to do with productivity, perhaps growth, reducing costs or maximizing profits. The moment you aren't useful in helping an organization to reach those goals, you can be dispensed with. You will be dispensed with. If your organization decides that it could reach its goals by replacing you or making you redundant, do you think for one moment that it would have any compunction about doing so?

Of course not. Which leads us on to the next fact. *Fact 2: The only person with responsibility for your career is you.* Don't expect your employers to look after you – you are little more than a resource to them. You are the only person who can manage your career, success, and happiness. It's up to you to ensure your own survival at work, creating allies and fending off enemies. Unless you're happy drifting aimlessly, it's up to you to set a course and steer your career in the right direction. You're the boss. Take control.

Fact 3: Shit happens. Organizational life is rarely "fair." Management doesn't promote individuals just because they "worked hard" or "deserved" it. Colleagues form cliques, pass the buck and pick on others in order to feel better about themselves. Honesty is rarely the best policy and hard work gets you nowhere. I know, I know, there are a few organizations that aren't like that – but most are.

Thankfully though, you can influence how much of that shit happens to you. Which leads us onto our final fact.

Fact 4: People with more political influence do better than those with less of it. Political influence delivers results. Political influence often trumps a good argument, beats what's in the best interests of the business. People with more political influence often get promoted over those with less of it;

they get invited to work on sexier projects and generally have an easier working life too.

Political influence takes many shapes and forms – you can have it if people like you or respect you, owe you a favor or even fear you. Make sure you accumulate as much political influence as you can. So these are the four facts of organizational life. Four principles that underlie everything else in this book. Don't forget them.

Sit back and enjoy the show

Years ago I worked with an office manager who laughed a lot. She had a loud, engaging, slightly flirtatious laugh. But, strangely, she laughed most at jokes made by the directors who owned the business. She didn't seem to find the jokes of the mere consultants or the lowly support staff quite as funny. But I have to give credit where it's due – her tactics made her popular with those in charge and allowed her to get away with behavior that would have got anyone else fired.

Start to develop your political awareness by looking out for different types of politically motivated behavior. Watch your colleagues' behavior in dealing with you and each other.

Look out for signs of destructive politicking such as:

- *Insincerity* – which can take many forms. Insincere and overly enthusiastic laughter at jokes made by people in authority is only one form of insincere behavior. Other forms include agreement with people in authority, flattery, or outright obsequiousness.
- *Misdirection* – lies, deceptions, and cover-ups are common at work when people behave in ways that they shouldn't.
- *Secrecy* – some individuals believe that power lies in having information and ideas that others do not. So don't be surprised if individuals or even entire departments hoard information and try to keep you in the dark.
- *Backstabbing and blame* – some individuals try to make themselves look good by making others look bad. Look out for malicious gossip, criticism and rumor-mongering that tries to make you or others look bad.
- *Favoritism* – certain individuals just seem to have been anointed by managers as successors or future leaders. Every boss has a favorite. Be sure to spot the favorites and figure out how you could become one too.

Take mental note of the tactics employed around you. Who is doing what? What exactly are they doing or saying to gain influence? And are they managing to get away with it? Watch, listen, absorb. Now is not yet the time for action. Sit back and enjoy the show.

Hear it on the grapevine

When a big bank recently announced that they would be cutting nearly two in three of their branch managers, the news was a huge shock to most of their loyal managers. But it came as little surprise to a select group who had already heard as much on the grapevine. A few of the more politically savvy managers had already secured transfers to other parts of the banking behemoth; a few more had begun to talk to headhunters, stealing a six-week advantage on the job market over the rest of their peers.

The grapevine is a source of competitive advantage. People who are plugged into the gossip, rumor, and innuendo of organizational life learn useful information. If you can figure out what direction everyone else is going in, you can decide whether you want to head in that direction too.

Of course, the foolish believe everything they hear, whereas in truth the grapevine is mainly filled with rubbish. For example, there has been a rumor going around a leading British airline that a new "open skies" agreement was about to be signed imminently, allowing them to fly from London Heathrow directly to the United States, and heralding a new era of growth and opportunity. Unfortunately, the rumor has been going around for over ten years.

Remember that people distort the truth too – sometimes unintentionally, perhaps through a haze of emotions or having misremembered the details. But many people quite deliberately exaggerate too – perhaps wanting to sound more dramatic or to elicit more sympathy. So be careful about acting on what they tell you.

But you are a bright enough person to be able to separate out the kernels of truth from the piles of untruths. Is the rumor being spread by just one source or many? Have those sources been accurate in the past or do they have a track record of believing and spreading idle speculation? What might their hidden agendas be for spreading lies?

Become a confidant

Deep down, everyone likes to talk. Everyone likes to vent their frustrations, talk up their successes, laugh at a silly mistake. And in getting to grips with the political landscape, there is no better tool than encouraging your colleagues to spill their innermost thoughts.

Work on showing your genuine interest in people. Find out their hopes and dreams, worries and fears. What are their day-to-day frustrations and long-term plans?

As you develop a bond, encourage them to spill the beans on the rest of your colleagues too. Most people enjoy talking about other people almost as much as they enjoy talking about themselves. Perhaps they take pleasure in sharing other people's secrets and stories because it makes them feel important. Maybe they are happy to tell all out of revenge, jealousy, or spite. More often than not, people just like to share an intrigue and feel for a moment more like a spy or undercover agent than a dreary office worker. It really doesn't matter what makes them want to share so long as they do.

Of course just about any occasion can be an opportunity to mine for information. Sharing a taxi back to the office from a client meeting. Sitting in a meeting room and waiting for the rest of the team. But the best opportunities are when your colleagues' guards are down – when they are tired, drunk, annoyed, or unhappy.

Whatever the circumstances, learn to be sympathetic. Be encouraging, solicitous, enthusiastic, whatever it takes. Learn to turn up at the right moment when they want to talk. Make it your mission to become a friend and confidant.

Shut up and listen!

You're probably thinking that you have pretty decent listening skills already. Most of us think we do. Just as most of us believe we're good drivers and great lovers. But listening intently is something that can be taken for granted all too easily. We let our minds drift and ... Sorry, what were you saying?

I'm sorry if this sounds really obvious. But surveys repeatedly do tell us that 99.99999 percent of employees feel that they don't get listened to. That they aren't appreciated enough. Okay, so I made that particular statistic up. But whether it's 70 percent or 80 percent or whatever, you can ingratiate yourself by showing that you really are listening, that you really do care.

I admit that a lot of the time your colleagues may be talking rubbish. You probably aren't really interested in their low-carbohydrate diet/new curtains/recent yoga retreat/groin operation. But savvy people shut up and listen because it turns you into their best friend.

Even if you aren't interested, at least pretend by using "active listening" cues. Lift your eyebrows and "flash" your eyes occasionally to signify that you understand what is being said. Nod intermittently to encourage them to continue or nod slowly in a sage-like fashion to indicate that you agree with what is being said. Use verbal cues such as "uh-huh," "mmm," and "yes" to reassure them that you are hanging on their every word.

Effective office politicians don't just listen dispassionately to the facts, but allow themselves to be drawn in by the emotions of people too. Make sure that you mirror their expressions, show your empathy. Your face should say, "I'm horrified at how badly your boss treats you" even if you are thinking, "I'm surprised your boss hasn't already fired you." Even when they are talking about nothing in particular, use these cunning listening cues to show that you are rapt by their every word.

Ask incisive questions

People don't always tell you what you want to know. Even when they are in full flow, confessing their sins or spilling their secrets, they might move off the topic or stop because they realize they have said too much. And that's when you need to encourage their momentum by asking a carefully placed question or two.

Avoid asking closed questions at all costs. If a question could be answered with a simple "yes" or "no," you might very well close off further avenues of interrogation ... er, exploration.

And remember that your role is to ask questions. Never, ever to pass judgment on what is being said. No matter how ridiculous or unreasonable they sound, resist the urge. It is not your job to pour cold water on their dreams, no matter how unrealistic. It is not for you to hand them the solution, no matter how obvious it might seem to you. Most of the time people only want sympathy, not advice. They want to be able to moan and complain, to vent their frustrations and feel that at least one other person understands them. There might be a time and place for solutions, but people rarely want advice. Even when people ask for opinions, what they really want is to be told how unfairly they have been treated and not how stupid they are being.

So ask questions. But keep them simple. Less is

more and all that. I find that two simple questions are often all that is needed to prod someone in the right direction. "What happened next?" and "Why?" can be said in just about any tone of voice to suit most occasions. Try saying it while sounding surprised or shocked, concerned or disappointed. You'll be amazed at how these two simple questions said in different tones of voice can allow you access to most inner thoughts.

Take careful note

Justin is a relationship manager in the world of private banking. He schmoozes wealthy clients over lengthy lunches and dinners in the hopes of investing their millions. On one occasion a meeting with a client was going badly. The client was stony faced and unimpressed with Justin's recommendations. Until Justin switched tactics and asked about the client's wife. In particular, was her health improving? Immediately the client melted, gushing about his wife's returning vigor. Anyway, to cut a long story short, Justin made a lot of money that day.

Now Justin admits to having an atrocious memory for detail. So he takes assiduous notes on both clients and colleagues. And he had noted that this client's wife was suffering from Lyme disease. Among other things he had in his notes were his predilection for Nicaraguan cigars, the names of his children, and the date of their next wedding anniversary (their 37th). All of which helped him to treat his client more as a friend than a business acquaintance.

Human memory is distinctly fallible. But the canny office politician cannot afford to be fallible. So. Keep track of the hot buttons and histories, the aspirations and foibles of your colleagues and clients.

However, I do say take careful note. Because people are curious if not downright nosey by nature. If exposed, your notes could be used as evidence against you, to prove your Machiavellian and scheming nature.

While a client is unlikely to have access to your computer, your colleagues will. Suspicious colleagues do go through folders and files on each other's hard drives. Remember that when you "delete" a file, it usually gets transferred to a recycle bin. Personally I keep important information in a spreadsheet locked with an alphanumeric password. And bear in mind that your employer's laptop ultimately belongs to them and not you. Be careful.

Use gossip with care

Absorb gossip about other people, but think twice before passing it on.

"Oh, didn't you know that Jane is three months' pregnant?" might be used by a colleague in the same sentence as commenting how tired and irritable she seems to be these days. Maybe it would be better not to put her on any interesting or challenging projects for a while?

"Don't tell anyone I told you this, but Peter is getting promoted" will almost certainly be used to imply that he didn't deserve it but is being promoted anyway.

Gossip undermines other people's credibility. But don't turn your nose up at the mere mention of it. Don't automatically refuse to listen to scurrilous rumors. Say that you're not interested in the game of corporate whispers and you will appear self-important. Even completely untrue rumors and tittle-tattle serve a purpose. In one of my previous employers, there was a rumor that our esteemed Chairman was dying his greying hair and another report that one of our (male) colleagues was partial to a "back, sack and crack" wax. Neither was probably true, but engaging in a little banter was a bonding strategy. It allows you to show that you can share a joke; it makes others warm to you and like you.

Gossip is fine – so long as people aren't gossiping about you. But be careful about using it. Yes, mentioning to a colleague that Jane is pregnant might help to sideline her and allow you to assume responsibility for that high-profile project. But can you imagine the fallout if she ever found out that you had spread word of her pregnancy? One instant enemy coming right up. Oh and imagine if it turned out that she hadn't been pregnant at all.

So listen to gossip, show your interest in it, and even laugh at the targets of the gossip. Even pass it on occasionally so long as you think through the potential consequences. Just never allow yourself to be identified as its source.

Learn to keep secrets

Telling people that I'm a psychologist often has a strange effect on them. Almost instantly they want me to analyze their dreams or body language. They confess secrets about their career plans, the team-mates they loathe, and their adulterous affairs. You name it and I have probably heard it.

While gossip is frivolous, secrets have true power. Secrets are truths that an individual decides to tell (or unwittingly reveals to) you. As such, they allow you a certain sway over the teller.

Let's say a colleague tremulously reveals to you that he is gay. If you are the tenth person he has told, then he's practically an out and proud man (whether he likes it or not). Which means that there are possibly ten confidants all trying to wend their way into his good books by being supportive. But if you are the only person he has told, then you have been entrusted with the opportunity to create a very special, personal rapport by being supportive. Asking you to keep a secret is akin to asking you a huge favor. And huge favors eventually need repaying.

So when you are told a secret, express your joy, surprise, amazement, or concern – but never allow yourself to pass it on.

As a trusted confidant, you have a special level of influence over that person so long as you keep the secret. But you lose it the moment you spill it to anyone else. Do you imagine that whoever told you their secret would trust you again if they found out you had shared their deepest, darkest secret with even one single other person?

We expect others to keep our secrets. Dedicate yourself to keeping them too.

Understand that perception is reality

One of my colleagues used to think that she was a tough-but-fair manager who ran her team efficiently and effectively. Unfortunately for her, the rest of us thought she was a domineering bully with borderline psychopathic tendencies who ruled her team by belittling and threatening others. Unsurprisingly, she didn't progress much further in her career because she couldn't understand how others – including the senior managers – perceived her.

How people are perceived governs how others will behave towards them. If someone is seen as arrogant, it doesn't matter if that poor person sees themselves as warm and approachable. If you are seen as gullible, then for all intents and purposes you are gullible – no matter how thrusting and dynamic you believe yourself to be.

Find out how others see you, how they think and feel about you. But don't make it an over-elaborate exercise. Just catch colleagues, clients and contacts during quiet moments and ask for their opinion. Explain that you think others in the team might think of you as disorganized or arrogant or gullible or whatever else you want to say. And encourage your colleague to pass comment.

Not that I believe we can eliminate all our weaknesses. Our weaknesses are areas in which much effort is required to produce little return. The trick is to work around them. Play to your strengths rather than worrying about your weaknesses. Avoid certain situations rather than beat yourself up for not excelling at everything.

It doesn't matter how you figure out what others perceive as your weaknesses. Only that you do it. Because in a world in which perception trumps reality, you need to ensure that you have crystal clarity on exactly how you are perceived.

Figure out what matters

Listen, hard work won't get you anywhere. In fact, working "hard" will only tire you out and make you feel frustrated that you aren't getting ahead. So don't do it.

Alex, a manager within an IT consultancy, was looking to be made up to a full partner within the business. He did great client work and was universally recognized as one of the most technically proficient and hardest working consultants within the office. But he was never invited to join the partnership. Because what mattered most in that consultancy was not doing good client work but finding new clients. Alex's problem was that, by nature, he was a "minder" – a good manager of existing clients – but not a "finder" of new clients.

In the glamorous world of magazine publishing, Karina was working up to 70 hours a week as an editorial assistant in the hopes of being promoted to edit her own section of a magazine. She was acknowledged as being diligent, but she was a "grinder" – someone who was good at the technical discipline of editing magazine content. But she needed to be a "minder" who could manage journalists and contributors.

Grinders are grunts, "the staff." Minders are supervisors, managers. Finders are Rainmakers, bringing in the money. The grinder/minder/finder distinction is a simplistic one. But in general minders are more valued than grinders. And, in turn, finders are more valued than minders.

As you scrutinize your colleagues, try to figure out how people really get promoted. Your organization may value some skills over others. Perhaps moving up to the next rung on the ladder might involve paying more attention to cost reduction or innovation, coaching or strategic planning.

But often the problem is not that people don't understand what it takes to get ahead. The problem is they enjoy what they currently do and don't relish the prospect of what they need to do. Becoming a minder means leaving behind the day-to-day job to spend more time delegating to others and managing the bigger picture. Transforming yourself from minder into finder involves getting out, interacting with more people, networking more.

Someone once coined the phrase "work smart, not hard." Trite but true. Don't just work hard in the hopes of being promoted. Don't get bogged down in the day-to-day nature of your job. Think about what you should be working on to get ahead.

What matters in your organization? And why aren't you doing it?

Find out who matters

We all know that not everyone has equal power and stature at work. Even two people with identical job titles rarely have the same clout. But it's your job to spot the folk who do have sway, power, influence.

Because unless you are the chief executive, the reality of working life is that you can't simply take what you want – you need to build relationships with other people and make them like you or respect you enough that they will give you what you want.

And of course a good working relationship

with someone who matters is going to get you further than one with someone who doesn't. You only have 24 hours in the day and I assume you might want to do stuff like eat, sleep, and spend time with the family occasionally. So you need to prioritize whom you choose to get to know at work. Make sure you can spot the players among the purists.

Purists are people who focus on their work. They dislike politics and try to work hard. They may be very good at their jobs and work honestly and diligently – if somewhat naively. They follow rules and regulations, trying to do what is "fair" or "right" and feel frustrated when decisions are not "fair" or "right." They are nice guys, but I'm afraid nice does not mean nice, it means loser. And because they refuse to play politics – seeing it as cronyism – purists get taken advantage of. They end up as organizational martyrs, moaning about the unfairness of life but never doing anything about it.

Players are the very opposite of purists. While they respect official rules and regulations, they understand that the unofficial rules of politics are often more important. They realize that decisions are rarely "fair" or "right" and that decision makers have personal as well as professional buttons that need to be pressed. Okay, they may not always be the very best at their day-to-day jobs, but their connections and influence help them to vault up the career ladder over their purist colleagues.

Purist or player? Player or purist? It's your choice.

It always amazes me that so many people refuse to play the political game at work. And in some utopian future in which we are all noticed for our skills and achievements we wouldn't have to. But until then, be sure to spot the players. Identify them, watch and learn.

Cut up your colleagues

No, I'm not proposing you take a knife to your rivals. I'm suggesting you segment and classify them further. While players are more important than purists, it stands to reason that a senior player is more important than a junior one too. So let's take the categorizing of your colleagues one step further to identify the movers and shakers within your organization.

Of course the chairman, chief executive and board are pretty important, but if you work in a large organization, they may simply be too far removed for you to try to get to know and influence them.

Focus instead on the colleagues and managers you could realistically spend time with. Think about people at your own level, as well as those perhaps two levels above and two levels below too.

Draw up a two-by-two grid and try to assign the names of your colleagues to one of the four quadrants of the grid depending not only on their level of influence (on the horizontal axis) but also their seniority (on the vertical axis).

As you populate the grid with names, try to think of each axis as a continuum. So place people who are two levels more senior than you higher up the vertical axis than those who are only a single level more senior. And people who have lots of influence should be further along to the right of the horizontal axis than those who have just a bit (see Figure 1).

The more discerning among you might notice that the grid bears a resemblance to the fabled BCG Matrix so beloved of MBA courses. Apologies to BCG for appropriating the idea and applying it to politicking at work!

	Low influence (purists)	High influence (players)
More senior than you	3. Has-beens	1. Bigwigs
Less senior than you	4. No-hopers	2. Rising stars

Seniority

Influence

Figure 1. Cutting up your colleagues

Focus on the few

Unless you are an incredibly unobservant person, you will have noticed that the political terrain is littered with oblivious, ineffective people. But the grid allows you to quickly identify individuals who are likely to be of use in assisting with your career goals.

Let's start with the important people first. The people who fall into the top right quadrant – the Bigwigs that are more senior to you and who possess more influence – are of course the ones you should aspire to develop the strongest relationships with. But even within that quadrant, the people who are in the uppermost and furthest right corner will be of the very greatest use.

Rising stars possess influence but perhaps have yet to be promoted. They deserve some attention from you and it is always useful to have these junior people on your side, as they may be able to access sources of gossip and information that your more senior contacts may not.

Has-beens have probably risen as far as they are going to because they don't really understand what they need to do to get ahead. They probably spend a lot of time moaning about how they are undervalued. The irony is that if they just complained a little less and worked a bit harder at building the right relationships, they would do better – but they probably don't like the idea of having to play political games. So they are stuck where they are.

Finally, the No-hopers probably don't even realize that there is a game to be played. Avoid spending too much time with either of the latter two categories as associating with them may be more of a drain on your resources than you will be able to recoup from them.

But never fall into the trap of ignoring entirely or being rude to Has-beens or No-hopers. Just because they are on the wane doesn't mean that they have no influence. Rudeness and abuses of power are rarely forgotten and have ways of being reported back to people who do matter. You may be a high flier with your sights on the top. But no matter how high you fly, remember that the grid merely points out who you should be extra nice to – not who you can be rude to.

Map the web of relationships

Identifying the key players in your organization is a good start. But key players do not sit in isolation. They interact with each other, forming a complex web of relationships. And it is only when you unravel who has sway with whom that you can establish how to get your way.

I heard from a business consultant, David, who explained his route to promotion. He had tried many and varied attempts to gain favor with the current managing director, but there was something about their chemistry that just didn't click. However, the MD frequently sought the counsel of one of the other board members. So David turned his attentions to impressing the other director. Word eventually got back to the MD about his sterling work. And he's now doing very nicely for himself, thank you very much.

Don't confuse the official hierarchy and formal reporting lines with where the real relationships lie. Of course a manager has to do what his boss says. But that doesn't mean that the manager will invest any more effort than is strictly necessary. No, the real relationships are driven by informal links, by friendships, common goals and common enemies, alliances and allegiances.

Sometimes the signs of proper relationships can

be apparent to everyone; I've known colleagues who share everything from lunches and drinks to babysitters and holidays together. But more usually the signs are understated – for example board members who tend to vote in a similar direction. Or colleagues who seem to linger around the water cooler. Even observing who chooses to sit next to each other in meetings could be a subtle indicator of who gets on with whom.

Build a mental map of who has sway with whom. If direct attempts to influence one person fail, try indirect attempts to influence around them. Enough said.

Uncover the secret rules

Every year, the senior partners from a top law firm gather in the gleaming boardroom of their London headquarters to discuss who will get invited to join the hallowed ranks of the partnership. An invitation means success, prestige, a big fat pay packet. Those who do not get invited often quit rather than face the shame. And the difference between promotion and rejection often comes down to whether the candidates "fit." "Yes, he fits." "Yes, she fits." "No, there's something about him that just doesn't fit."

"Fit" is an elusive, almost mystical quality, but every organization has secret rules that govern how people need to behave to fit in and succeed. The secret rules are about the organization's culture, its modus operandi, the way things happen around here. These rules are implicit, never written down, rarely even alluded to. Many of your colleagues may not even realize that they exist. But if you behave in line with these elusive rules, you fit; if you break the rules, you don't fit. It's as simple as that.

In trying to fathom out the secret rules, don't get taken in by what managers say you need to do. What they openly promote is rarely the same as what they secretly want.

Take a certain European technology firm. It publicly proclaims how it aims to partner with customers and consider their needs above all others. But in reality you'll never get promoted into a senior position unless you are happy to manipulate the truth and occasionally tell barefaced lies to customers in order to win orders and grow revenues.

Elsewhere, no one will ever write it down that you need to go out drinking with your buddies from the office, perhaps getting uproariously drunk a couple of times a month and then visiting a lap dancing club. But don't do it and you will get left behind at a certain American investment bank.

At another firm, managers who make it to the top rarely do so without moderating their language, throwing dinner parties where bringing a socially respectable partner is de rigueur, and publicly developing interests in the fine arts.

Here's the point. Keep watch on the successful people, listen carefully, notice what counts. And emulate what they do, how they do it. Because what people do when they sit down at their desks is never what it takes to get ahead. It's about how they sell to customers, how they pitch ideas to colleagues, how they bond with their peers. About how they liaise between departments, how they arrange deals, how they create a profile with Bigwigs. Never confuse the written rules with the secret rules.

Delve deeper into the secret rules

As you strive to understand the secret rules of your organization, consider some of the following questions:

- To what extent are directness and honesty really appreciated? Almost every organization claims that it encourages its employees to speak up. But in some places smart employees know that voicing overly honest opinions will mark them out as troublemakers. It's the corporate equivalent of your partner asking "Do I look fat in this?" Consider carefully whether your colleagues really want to hear a truth or a platitude.

- How much socializing must you do with colleagues? Some organizations are happy to let employees keep their work lives separate from their personal ones. But others – often bigger and/or American firms – actively encourage employees to get together over lunches and dinners, drinks and even bonding weekends. In certain organizations, the really important decisions are as likely to be made over a cognac and cigar as in a meeting room. Make sure you are sufficiently sociable for your organization.

- What's the organization's view on risk? Most organizations say that they encourage employees to be creative and take risks, but few actually mean it. Most organizations would like to be innovative, but end up penalizing risk takers. So consider how your organization treats people who take risks and try to be innovative. Are they celebrated or punished?

- To what extent do people bend official rules and regulations? For example, managers in public sector organizations or those in dangerous industries such as oil and gas often stick to rules to the point of appearing bureaucratic and inflexible. On the other hand, managers in professional services firms sometimes appear just a little too willing to bend the rules to get the job done. Does your organization believe that ends justify means? Or does it believe that means and ends are equally important?

- How should you dress? Perhaps it sounds stupidly obvious, but clothing is often the most visible indicator of whether you fit. In one large media business, you can almost always tell someone's standing in the hierarchy by the way they dress. Torn jeans and just-got-out-of-bed hair? Then they're a runner or researcher. Smart designer jeans and designer t-shirt? Then you must be a producer. Suit? Well, executives wear smart suits while accountants wear cheap ones.

Behaving in line with your organization's secret rules doesn't automatically mean that you will succeed. But take my word for it that flaunting them will certainly scupper your chances.

Recognize that bosses are blind

I met a top hotelier recently at a charity drinks reception. I mentioned that I was on the lookout for examples of politicking for this book. He said that he hated office politics and told me emphatically that there were no politics in his office. I tried not to laugh in his face – it seemed ungracious given that he was hosting the event at his lovely hotel. But it seemed deathly ironic to me as I watched his minions scurrying around him, keeping half an eye on the guests while trying at the same time to suck up to the boss man and whoever he was talking to as much as humanly possible. And nowhere was this more apparent than in watching his two aides – one an executive assistant and the other a mere personal assistant – vie for attention with each other.

Almost all bosses are blind to the politics that go on beneath them. Because for them to recognize that the team, department or entire organization under them is rife with politics is to admit that they have failed to create an egalitarian place to work. Even middle and junior managers usually believe that the organization is only political for people at their level and above.

So politics is a game that must never be mentioned. Tell your boss about internal politics in their team and you won't get a happy response. You may as well accuse him or her of having favorites and being unable to manage the team. Play the game – just don't talk to your boss about it.

Trust your instincts

Ever get the feeling that something is wrong but can't put your finger on it exactly? Everything I've talked about so far in assessing the political landscape makes it sound like a very considered and controlled process of observing and analyzing. And for the most part it is. But it doesn't mean that your instincts and intuition have absolutely no part to play in judging what goes on around you too.

When it comes to observing how people behave, communication between humans is amazingly complex. Over 90 percent of the meaning that we get from our interactions from other people comes not from what they say but how they say it. Pitch, tone, and pausing all conspire to transmit messages that speakers do not intend to reveal; body language often betrays true feelings that might otherwise go unspoken.

So even though you may sometimes have no good reason to suspect or believe something, you might want to anyway. If something looks or sounds odd, then you might be right to tread carefully. If you don't like someone but can't figure out why, it may just be that your brain hasn't quite put all of the facts together yet.

Here's the science bit. Brain research shows that we may engage in something called traverse processing. These thought processes are subconscious, but not necessarily irrational. Sometimes we can't access how or why we came to a conclusion, but it doesn't mean that it isn't based on some kind of factual processing. At times our subconscious might be reading body language signals that are more intricate and subtle than the conscious brain can interpret.

So in reading the rules of office politics, don't ignore your instincts and intuition entirely. Trust yourself. Trust your judgment.

Take your time

Okay, you may have noticed that a group of your colleagues go drinking most Tuesdays. But rather than immediately trying to involve yourself with them and be included in their little crowd, step back to consider whether they might be the right colleagues to be associated with. Are they seen as a group of influential Rising Stars or nobodies?

Political savvy is not accomplished overnight. People are slow to impress, but make the wrong move and they are quick to rile. Rush into the political arena with an imperfect understanding of how to behave and you could ruin your chances. Especially if you are joining a new organization, don't try to play the politics until you have invested at least several months in quiet observation and analysis.

While the rest of your colleagues throw themselves at the feet of the wrong people or at the right people but in the wrong way, allow yourself the luxury of doing nothing. Sit back and identify the key players – the Bigwigs and the Rising Stars. And take your time to check that they really are the Bigwigs and Rising Stars. Bear in mind that some people are full of bluster and seeming confidence, but in reality command far less respect from their colleagues and influence with them than they claim.

Remember too that all of your colleagues have their own personal agendas and flaws. Some may deliberately feint left but go right, telling you one thing while behaving very differently. Others may misinform you not for malicious reasons but simply because they know no better.

So put up your metaphorical feet and watch the show. Imagine that you are a scientist, watching animals in their natural habitat. Identify the different varieties of beast, establish their behavioral patterns. Seek the opinions of trusted colleagues but always use your own judgment and be careful about revealing your true intentions.

Beginning your political campaign with only half an understanding of the political landscape could be fatal – to your career if not to your actual life. So s-l-o-w d-o-w-n. Observe, analyze, understand, and categorize. Only then will you be ready to act.

BUILDING SIGNIFICANT RELATIONSHIPS

A while back, I worked in a consulting firm in which one of the directors recommended a particular consultant, Nadine, for promotion. Along with several other candidates, Nadine was put through an assessment center. And she passed. One of the assessors later confided that she hadn't really been that impressive. But I'm sure it was just a coincidence that Nadine was the younger sister of the director who recommended her. I'm sure everything was above board.

We've all heard it before. It's not what you know, it's who you know. And that is as true now as it was 50 years ago. Of course family ties at work would help, but you don't have to have them to achieve your goals. Anyone can build their own ties, cultivate relationships, find allies, create friendships even. More often than not, it's people who can choose to help or hinder you in achieving your goals. And it's relationships with them that will ensure they help rather than hinder.

But what exactly are your goals? Of course, most people want to be "more successful" in their careers. But what exactly does "success" mean for you? Establishing a set of career goals will help you to focus the ways you spend your time and energy. Only when you know what you want can you start to think about who and how to influence to get it.

It's all very well identifying the people you

need to influence. But why should they help you? What's in it for them?

I say that effective politicking is about building relationships. But there are relationships and then relationships. You may know some senior managers well enough to exchange hellos in the lift. But do you know them well enough to understand what drives them, makes them happy, worries or terrifies them? Do you know them well enough to know how to be helpful to them? To build goodwill and a sufficient depth of relationship to be able to call on their help in return?

The more you understand the key people around you, the more effectively you will be able to influence them. And that's what this part of the book is about.

Identify your goals

So what are your goals? Most people don't have any. I bet most of your colleagues live their lives on a day-to-day basis. You probably hear them moan about their jobs and how undervalued they feel. They keep their fingers crossed about winning the lottery, hoping for dumb luck to sort out their lives. They wish and dream, but resign themselves to their dreary lives, knowing that wishes and dreams rarely come true.

Smart people don't rely on luck. They don't just hope, pray, wish, or dream. They set goals, establish a direction. They set goals and work on turning them into a reality.

Now some of you might argue that you already have a set of goals in the shape of a personal development plan (PDP). But think about it for a moment. A PDP is basically a document telling you how you will strive to develop yourself in ways that benefit the organization. PDPs tackle your weaknesses and try to make you a better member of the team.

Your personal goals probably have little to do with the goals that your manager has signed off for you in your PDP. You don't admit to stuff like wanting to set up your own business, wanting to raise a family, or wanting your boss's job. Identifying your personal goals is about thinking about what you want for yourself. Remember that your organization would happily toss you aside if it could improve its bottom line. So. Be selfish and think about yourself for a change.

Picture where you want to be in five or ten years' time. Your goal may be do with rapid promotion, running a big team, a department, the entire business. Perhaps you want to get that corner office with the nice view. Maybe you want to make change happen, draw attention to an important cause, raise funds for a favored charity. Or maybe you want to reduce your hours and improve your work–life balance. Your goals are personal to you. No one else can tell you what is right or wrong. Just make sure you have some goals.

I once read on a Chinese fortune cookie: "Without a clear goal, how do you expect to score?" It sounds like it was written by a moon-lighting copywriter rather than a sage old Chinese philosopher, but it's essentially true – you can't reach a goal unless you have one.

Don't carry on reading until you have identified your goal. Put the book down and ponder for a bit. What do you want out of your life? And what do you really hope to achieve in your career? They're big questions, but your goals should ultimately be about what makes you happy.

Unless you want to waste your life hoping, dreaming and wishing, identify your goals. Do it. Now.

Devise a cunning plan

A goal is your destination, where you want to be. But a plan is the road map that will get you there. A goal can be lofty, grand, aspirational. But your plan has to be grounded in reality, the series of logical steps to carry you toward your goal.

Say you want to set up your own business. You might need investors, employees, a product. So who might be interested in investing? How will you find them? Where will you find employees or will you hire someone to do the recruiting for you? And what about the product – will you need someone to develop it with you or for you? That's already more than a handful of steps that will need to go into your plan. Along with time-frames to motivate you to get it done sooner rather than later.

In business, the right question is usually "Who?" rather than "How?" Dealing with the "how" is much easier if you have the right "who" to do it for you.

Let's take another example. You want a promotion. Well, what are the steps? Perhaps a transfer to another department to pick up new skills, relocation or a secondment for further career experience, or new qualifications. And who are the key decision makers? Your boss, HR, your boss's boss. There might also be people in other departments who could be willing to put in a word with your boss if you manage to impress them enough. So how will you influence each of them?

Take your ultimate goal and devise that cunning plan. Study people you respect and see how they did it. Work out the actions you need to take, the bite-sized tasks you need to complete.

Of course plans can't be set in stone. Perhaps

a new boss arrives on the scene, your personal life changes, or the organization goes through a restructure. As circumstances change, your plan has to change and adapt. The dinosaurs didn't adapt and look at them now. Plan and revisit your plan frequently. Tweak it and improve it, add to it and adjust it. So long as your momentum takes you forwards, you have a chance of turning your goals into a very satisfying reality.

Scheme without scheming

Schemers and plotters, that's what politically active people are usually called. Or at least that's how they are portrayed by colleagues envious of their success and speedy ascent up the organizational hierarchy. Politicking has such a tarnished image that it's never a good thing to be seen to be political. Acting politically is seen to be shouting about hollow achievements, undercutting rivals, using people. If you gain the reputation of being political, others will become more wary of you. So effective politicking must never stab others in the back or be manipulative.

Politically savvy individuals do plan. Rather than rushing around and spreading their efforts around too thinly, they look at the political land-scape and make decisions about whom, how, and why to influence in order to achieve their goals. Unfortunately your colleagues would undoubt-edly worry that such purposeful planning was nefarious, devious, and underhand. So don't mention your goals or plans to other people.

Nothing reminds your colleagues more of their own failure than seeing success in other people. Yes, there may be some people who will be genuinely happy for you to succeed. But for every one who is happy for you, there will be four others thinking that your success wasn't deserved.

You need to make your success look almost accidental. Maneuver carefully and never be blatant about it. Your aim is to create the impres-sion that you are a genuine, likeable individual. But the best way to create the impression that you are genuine and likeable is to be genuine and likeable. That should give you pause for thought as you put together your plans for world domination.

Remember there is no "I" in "team"

Organizations are forever reminding employees that they need to pull together and put the needs of the team first. And teamworking is great for organizations because it basically allows them to extract more hard work and productivity from employees. But putting the needs of the team ahead of your own needs isn't always the best idea when it comes to creating a successful and satisfying career.

The old management maxim about there being no "I" in "team" is completely true. And that's exactly why business historians never remember great teams. Can you name any of the members of the team who made Richard Branson arguably Britain's most famous business person? Or how about any of the team who worked for Jack Welch at GE or any other leader?

The point is that teams are good for one thing and one thing only – they are good for the organization. There's no "I" in the word "team" because teams aren't much use when it comes to advancing your personal goals.

When it comes to building useful relationships, remember that you are doing so to further your career goals. Don't overstretch yourself by trying to help others out too much. Stay focused on building relationships with those who are the most useful to you.

I'm not suggesting that you should manipulate people or be devious. Just prioritize how you spend your time. Don't be so self-sacrificing all of the time. Yes, there may be times when you do need to put the interests of others ahead of your own. But looking at the long-term game, put your own interests ahead of those of the team for a change. Of course you should never tell people that's what you're doing. But do it nonetheless.

Identify hot buttons

People are complex, frustrating, exasperating. Or at least until you figure out what makes them tick.

In one organization that I have come across, the Chairman is a self-made man who has grown his business over two decades of hard work and determination. But ideas from his team often fail to impress him – even when they clearly have merit for the business. The canny employees who succeed in driving projects through and reaping the career rewards realize that business benefit is only secondary; in order to succeed, proposals have to fan the flames of the Chairman's ego.

Business benefit without much fan-waving is always doomed to failure.

Neither is that business that unusual. I've mentioned that people rarely choose to make decisions based purely on what is in the best interests of the organization or what is "fair" or "right." More often than not, their decisions are tainted by their own personal agendas, their own little hot buttons that you must learn to press.

Of course, no one ever talks about their personal agendas. Instead everyone talks about wanting personal development and seeking challenges. But take a careful look at the people around you. What motivates them?

Money makes the world go around. Allegedly. But, perhaps surprisingly, many managers and executives actually crave recognition more than the cash itself. They chase money not because it allows them to buy things in the real world but because it accords them status and respect from their peers, their friends, their colleagues. In most organizations, there is an implicit perception that a bigger salary (or bonus or stock options and so on) means that you are more important, more worthwhile, a better person. The Chairman who needs fan-waving to impress him really wants recognition more than he wants money – even if he might not realize it himself. So be careful not to assume that just because some people seem to be financially fixated that they actually want the money itself – they might actually be trying to buy respect and appreciation.

Few managers and professionals pursue cash for its own sake. There are plenty of millionaire businesspeople who have built up businesses, sold them, and reaped the rewards. But then choose only to invest in another business and work to build that up. More often than not, they need the challenge, the recognition, the fun, and not the money itself.

What motivates the people around you?

Recognize common hot buttons

We all hate to be bossed around. But for certain people, they like nothing more than to be the boss. They need to feel in control of the lives of others as well as their own. They enjoy having authority and sway over others. They crave power and enjoy taking the lead over teams, departments or even entire organizations. Giving these people the opportunity to take charge makes them feel at their best. Make them feel that an idea was theirs and they will usually only too happily pursue it with dogged determination.

But there are many forces that drive people on. Consider some of the other alternatives too:

- *Personal growth.* While most people say they are looking for challenges, only a small number of individuals genuinely thrive on being presented with new challenges, accomplishing difficult tasks, and bettering themselves. They may not need the recognition of others or financial reward to motivate them. They enjoy the feeling of overcoming obstacles and learning from their experiences.

- *Social interaction.* Some people seem to possess an innate ability to work on their own, perhaps disliking or even fearing having to work with other people. Others, however, seem unable to function independently without wanting to chat or bounce ideas off others.

- *An easy life.* There are some people who want nothing more than a trouble-free existence at work. They want a job that pays them enough and gives them as little stress as possible. They want to arrive at 9 and leave at 5.

But just as others have hot buttons, so do you. Hot buttons are a way of encouraging, influencing, persuading people. And that goes both ways. What do others have to say or do to get

you on side or get around you? If you understand yourself, you can avoid letting others
manipulate you. Be careful.

Play to people's needs

I've spent years watching successful people. And
I've noticed that, above all, successful people are
social chameleons. They have a special talent for
pressing hot buttons subtly and giving people
what they want.

As you identify the needs of different people,
think about how it will allow you to influence
them more effectively. For someone who craves
social contact and participation, try emphasizing
how fun a task or project would be and how it
would allow you all to get to spend time together
and get to know each other. For someone who
abhors teamwork, find a way to let them work on
a chunk of the project with as little interference or
disturbance as possible.

For an obstructive colleague who needs
recognition, always present your ideas and
proposals in a way that accords them the respect
they desire. Even if accepting your proposals
might mean them having to back down, look for
a way for them to retain their dignity. Avoid

bragging about your success; show publicly your appreciation and thanks. Make them look the hero of the piece to ensure that they will aid you again in the future.

Or for someone who wants only an easy life, often the best way to motivate them into action is to worry them that the status quo is at risk of being broken. Hint that they might have to work harder or adopt new and possibly difficult ways of working – unless they respond to your call for action, of course.

Hot buttons are never on public display. You can't tell what drives someone until you get to know them, catch them when their guard is down, understand them. Come on, your colleagues aren't going to admit readily that they are unhappy in their private lives so make up for it by obsessing about their secret needs. That they need respect because they never got it when they grew up. Or that they really aren't that fussed about what goes on at work so long as they can get home on time. But if you know what's motivating a person, you can give it to them and turn them into an ally or even a friend. Find out what they need. And they will give you what you need.

Adapt your style

Whenever the Starship *Enterprise* gets hit by enemy phasers, someone on the bridge always yells that they are going to "modulate the shields." A true Trek-fan would know what it's supposed to mean, but I guess it's something to do with adapting to enemy fire. And the key to building strong relationships is to adapt your style in all of your interactions with people.

I used to work with two Bigwigs and it was a matter of career survival to modulate my shields when working with either of them. Bigwig Alistair liked to use the F-word. A lot. The traffic on the way in to the office was f-ing awful. The IT systems were usually f-ing slow. Of course clients were f-ing stupid. Bigwig Shaun was rather fond of talking and sharing innuendoes about women's breasts.

Now both Alistair and Shaun were complex human beings and had a lot to contribute apart from swearing a lot and being breast-fixated. But the members of the team who noticed these little foibles definitely got on with them better than the ones who either did not notice or could not bring themselves to adapt their styles. When Alistair was around, you'd swear more. When you were one-to-one with Shaun, a breast joke would never go amiss.

But it went further than that. One of my

colleagues seemed to flinch slightly whenever Alistair swore. Geoff felt uncomfortable with Alistair. And Alistair, sensing Geoff's discomfort, never warmed to Geoff. When the firm hit a bad patch and needed to make someone redundant, guess who got the chop?

The only problem is that some of what the Bigwigs in your organization do or say is bound to scrape up against your personal values. Swearing is offensive; joking about women's breasts is misogynistic. But it brings us back to the fact that organizational life is rarely "fair" or "right." Just be conscious that there will be times when you may need to choose whether to do what is right or what will help you to get you ahead.

A warning though. Don't start to adopt other people's mannerisms or accents wholesale. There's a big difference between adapting your style and mimicking and mocking. Do the former; don't do the latter.

Edit what you share with others

Back in the early days of my career, there was a colleague I didn't much like. She was a know-it-all, she was loud, she got drunk at client events. And I used to take great pleasure in bitching about her to anyone who would listen, but especially to my best friend and confidant at work. You probably know where this is headed. Yes, my best friend and my loathed colleague started seeing each other. In fact, they ended up getting married. Perhaps unsurprisingly, I lost my friend and ally.

Be careful what you give away, what you tell others. When you spend time with key individuals, soak up their information and news. But be careful what you give away, what you tell them in return.

However, I'm not advocating that you should be a completely closed book. If you don't share a little about yourself, people will think you odd, an enigma, inhuman.

As you delve further into people's insecurities, their foibles and failings, you have to appear will- ing to share some of your own in return. People only feel comfortable opening up when they feel that there is a reciprocal level of trust and sharing. A touch of vulnerability is endearing. After all, would you be happy to admit your faults to someone who seemed to have none?

Refusing to divulge some of the workings of your own mind can have even worse repercussions. Just as nature abhors a vacuum, human nature looks to fill the void with gossip and speculation. Others may wonder what you are hiding. And what they make up may be far worse than the truth.

But choosing to share some of your own weaknesses needs preparation on your part. Spontaneity is often the Achilles' heel of many a would-be office politician. A blurted-out story about too great a failing could be used by your enemies against you. Too minor a revelation might seem trite and inappropriate in comparison to some of the weighty issues that others choose to share with you. The wrong anecdote or story could make you sound whiney or bitter or bitchy. So, as my personal early failure should have demonstrated, choose carefully what you share.

Bank favors

Let's face it. A big part of politics involves mutual back-scratching. Scratch long and hard enough, and someone will feel obliged to hit that sweet spot of yours in return. Because political influence is a currency that you can earn by helping others out. Think of each favor you do as a deposit in a favor bank that you can later draw upon.

Like some sort of practical karma, you get what you give. Sometimes the favors you do for others need no understanding of their individual hot buttons. Busy people are always grateful for help in dealing with otherwise insurmountable workloads.

But often you can bank favors by understanding how to help different people. One person might want nothing more than a shoulder to cry on when a project goes badly. Another might need a detached, objective person to bounce an idea off. Yet another might shy away from all that touchy-feely nonsense and want nothing more than your enthusiasm and public support for a proposal that will help them to achieve a personal business goal.

The list goes on. Perhaps you could pass on a snippet of information, a timely warning, a piece of advice. Or an introduction to a new contact, a supplier, a headhunter. Even compliments are a favor of sort – you make a person feel good, boost their self-esteem for a mere moment, and they associate you with good feelings; they warm to you and become more responsive to you.

Never talk explicitly about the favors you are banking. When someone needs a kind word, the last thing they want to hear is that you are only spending time with them because you will call in the favor at a later date. You can be sure that's the route to instantly blowing any trust or relationship you may have built up.

Keep helping others out and making deposits within your favor bank. The more deposits you make, the bigger the eventual windfall you will be able to collect. But building political influence isn't a get-rich-quick scheme. Just as funds in a bank don't triple overnight, don't expect a few minor favors on your part to reap disproportionately large paybacks any time soon. Before you ask an individual for their undying support, make sure that you have put more than a handful of pennies into the favor bank. Be generous with your favors before you expect to see them returned.

Deepen personal relationships

But there's more to building useful relationships than constantly chasing after key individuals and doing favors for them. Throwing yourself at people and offering to help out in any way possible can smack of desperation or a transparent attempt to curry political favor. So here are two principles that will help you to cement those relationships.

The first is the principle of reciprocity. Relationships need to be two-sided. Do too much of the work and it will feel one-sided, unbalanced. So show your vulnerable side occasionally. Ask for help. Let others know when you feel tired or angry, overworked or unhappy. Of course do it selectively so you don't come across as a whining slacker. But do it enough to make others feel that you depend on them as much as they can depend on you.

The second is the principle of validation. People like to feel special. They want to believe that you are helping them because you like them, not because you need them. That you enjoy spending time with them, not because you have an end game. So look for ways to show your appreciation of them as individuals.

Consider their skills and abilities, personality traits and personal qualities. And look for ways to respect unique aspects of each person. While one person might be reliable and dependable when there's too much work on, another person may have analytical skills that are second to none. Others might have a sense of self-deprecation that is second to none or an optimism that is infectious. Try to validate other people by using language such as:

- "I always know I can depend on you for ..."
- "You're the only person I can trust to ..."
- "I knew no one else could ..."

Reciprocity and validation. Written down they probably sound trite, patronizing, simplistic. But executed well, they will generate unassailable relationships that will ultimately deliver what you want.

Play a long game

They say that patience is a virtue. And unfortunately they (whoever "they" are, answers on a postcard please) are right. Because political influence is not built overnight.

Sure, you might discover very quickly what drives a particular player or Bigwig. But understanding is only a prerequisite to political effectiveness. It's what you do with that understanding that builds political influence. For instance, learning that a particular Bigwig can't stand one of the other members of the management team isn't the same as removing that person for them. And building influence is a long game.

Sometimes you might be tempted to ask a favor even when you haven't made many deposits into the favor bank. You could try making a withdrawal based on goodwill and the promise of future favors. Just be explicit about it and don't be afraid to state what you are willing to do in return. But don't expect it to work on anything more than the most simple and undemanding of requests. Sure, someone might be willing to offer a few minutes of their time – but don't expect them to speak up in support of a controversial proposal unless you have saved up some serious favors first.

Keep track of the handful of key individuals with whom you want to build stronger and deeper relationships. Your two-by-two grid should throw up more than a handful, but start with just a few to begin with. Then look for ways to help each of them individually. If you leave it to spontaneity and chance, it won't happen. Think ahead and seek deliberate opportunities to help them overcome obstacles or pick them up emotionally when they feel down.

Unlock gatekeepers

I remember an ex-office mate of mine once banging the telephone down in frustration. I was a bit shocked because, although I hadn't heard the words, from his overly cheerful tone I'd assumed he had been speaking to one of his young children. But no, he had been speaking to the personal assistant of a client. And he had fallen into the trap of patronizing the assistant without realizing it.

Yes, one of the most frustrating phrases in the world is: "I'm sorry but he's busy at the moment – can I take a message?" But it's no excuse for rudeness.

When it comes to trying to deal with senior Bigwigs, beware of the gatekeeper. Secretaries, personal assistants, office managers, support staff, and executive assistants (the breadth of their titles is often nearly as numerous as the number of times you have to call to get past them) are often ruthlessly efficient at keeping scum like you from bothering their bosses.

They are paid to do pretty much whatever it takes – including telling lies that vary from little white ones to big fat whoppers – to protect their bosses. Ask any Bigwig and they will usually tell you (if you can actually manage to get past their gate-keeper to speak to them) that the good assistants are worth their weight in gold. A gatekeeper will often trawl through the boss's email inbox, physical mail, and telephone voicemail. Nothing gets through unless the gatekeeper deems it relevant.

Short of physically tackling them to the ground and bursting into the Bigwig's office, you will need to get gatekeepers on your side. Treat them like a mere lackey and you can guarantee that your requests will go to the bottom of the pile – if it even makes it to the pile rather than joining the rubbish in the waste bin. Just because you may earn three or four times what they do doesn't mean that you can talk down to them. Treat them as equals. Befriend them with an appropriate mix of humor, professional courtesy, and respect for their difficult job, and you might just get what you want.

Maintain a broad network

Yes there may be certain key players who count. But that doesn't mean they exist in a vacuum. Focusing your attention on only a handful of key individuals could give you too narrow a perspective on what's going on, leave you blindsided to important events and developments.

The office repair guy will see things the managing director won't. The receptionist will hear things none of the managers ever will. The more people you are on speaking terms with, the more likely you will find out useful news and information. The political landscape is a big place and you can't be everywhere at once. But a good network of contacts can act as your extended eyes and ears. The more diverse it is – consisting of people at all levels within, across, and even outside of the organization – the better.

Bear in mind that the people in your network are only useful so long as they have you at the forefront of their minds. Don't sit at your desk believing that you have a big network, because you probably don't. Time slips by quickly and contacts become ex-contacts, friends become mere acquaintances, at a startling pace. People have short memories and you could easily fall off their radars.

Make an effort to spend time with people. That's what lunch breaks and coffee breaks are for. Don't be one of those purists who say that they are too "busy" to go have lunch. Yes, taking a break may mean you get less of your current task done. But remember that success is not built by the completion of tasks but by the building of relationships.

Make it a priority to grab a 20-minute sandwich break with someone or sit on the corner of their desk and chat for a few minutes. Resist the urge to go back to the same few people, your close friends, your confidants, all the time. Seek contact with someone different daily. Doesn't matter whether you banter about the football results or the latest celebrity scandal. Just remember that having "too much work" to take a break is a sure sign that you are turning into the kind of narrow-minded purist who thinks that he or she can succeed through hard work alone.

Networks don't just happen. They develop

through conscious effort. What could you do tomorrow to broaden yours?

Seek a mentor

My father always tells me that it's the mistake of the young to believe they are doing it for the first time. I never want to listen to him, but when I do I (grudgingly) have to admit that he's usually right. So listen to Mr Yeung (senior).

One of the best ways to understand how the levers of power work in your organization is to seek a mentor. It helps if they are further up the hierarchy so they have a broader overview of organizational life than you. But what's more important is that they are experienced and have not only absorbed the organization's culture and ways of working, but can offer insight about it.

Many organizations institute formal mentoring programs. But formal programs are often about the development of management skills rather than the really important stuff about understanding culture and politics. And, more often than not, any mentor assigned to you may not have access to the inner workings of the organization. So make it your responsibility to seek a mentor.

Identify potential mentors and get to know their

background and track record. Perhaps approach then and say that they are where you want to be – perhaps in three or five years' time. Flatter them by explaining that you admire their success and would value their experience and insight. Tell them that you are ambitious and willing to learn.

Then ask your mentor why people succeed or fail in the organization. Encourage them to share tales of office savagery and political victory. Ask their opinion on the players in the organization and what they do or say that makes them successful. They know plenty about the culture, the secret rules. So listen and learn.

When your mentor knows you better, request candid feedback on your weaknesses. Ask for suggestions on how you should develop your skill set and network to improve your effectiveness and standing within the organization.

More practically, remember that your mentor is doing you a favor, giving of their precious time and thoughts. So always be solicitous. Be sure to be flexible. Mentoring meetings could at a push be conducted over the telephone as well as in person; they could be a half-hour in their office or over a lengthy lunch (where you, of course, pay).

Okay, do it now. Before moving on with the book, have a think: Who could mentor you?

Manage your reputation

I once worked alongside a famous television presenter. Blonde, talks a lot, wears a tad too much make-up. Plus a reputation for being a bit … demanding. You don't see her on television as much nowadays. Unsurprisingly, her reputation precedes her and television producers just aren't keen to work with her.

What's your reputation like?

How others see you drives their behavior. It's going back to the realization that perception is reality in the world of work. How people treat you is based on how others see you – and not how you actually are. They aren't telepathic – they can't read your mind – so have to rely instead on what they see and hear. The deluded television presenter probably thinks of herself merely as a woman who asserts her rights.

And you will pick up a certain reputation – good, bad, or indifferent – whether you actively manage it or not. If you do not craft one for your-self, you leave yourself vulnerable to having a reputation created for you.

The good news is that it doesn't matter if you are actually fairly bad at certain skills – so long as other people believe you are good at them.

Having spent time observing others, reading the culture and assessing the political terrain, it's time to manage your reputation. You've spotted what people say and do to get ahead. So now it's your turn. Start by adopting a handful of behaviors and phrases that you like from other people. It's not copying or stealing. In the world of work, it is called "benchmarking" and "sharing best practice." Watch the Bigwigs and Rising Stars and learn from how they behave.

If they go to charity events, you start next week. If they wear double-cuffed shirts, buy five tomorrow. If they obsess over the financials, you do it too.

There are entire books written on the topic of reputation. But they can be summed up very simply: Behave as the person you want to be. It doesn't matter if you aren't a senior manager yet. Talk, dress, and behave like one and the rest will follow.

Develop your profile

Two candidates recently applied for a senior management role. One was more experienced and had a better track record of results. But the other got the job, with the Powers That Be saying that he had more "potential." No one knew exactly what that meant. But it probably had little to do with burying his head in his work and everything to do with being noticed, becoming memorable, and raising his profile.

Doesn't matter how good you are unless people know it. Unseen contributions have little or no political value. Of course purists hate the idea that you must have a profile to succeed. But, again, that's just the way the organizational cookie crumbles.

Alan was a very successful area manager for a high street bank, managing around 20 branches and hundreds of staff. He wanted the next job up, but despite having great results year after year after year, it wasn't happening. He said that he preferred to let his results speak for themselves. But the results plainly weren't saying enough.

Because at the bank the Bigwigs wanted more than mere results. They wanted leaders with presence, impact, promise, charisma. So we hatched a plan for Alan to give the Bigwigs what they wanted. He cut back on the number of days he spent at branches and instead spent an extra two days a month at head office. Under the guise of "sharing new ideas," "benchmarking" and "communicating best practice," he wormed his way onto the Bigwigs' radars. Pick up the tale a year later and Alan is now a regional director with nearly 25 areas, 400 branches, and thousands of staff reporting to him.

The lesson is straightforward. Look for ways to raise your profile. Speak up in key meetings. Put yourself forward and volunteer for cross-departmental initiatives and change projects. Send out email missives with news worthy of celebration. Create new processes and procedures for others to use. If you have a way of working that could save others time or effort, then share it and highlight your efforts. Tell people you exist and remind people of what you can do.

Be prepared for opposition

Pick up a newspaper or turn on the television and you'll find what passes for news is usually bad news. People want to hear about disasters and tragedies or the rich and famous being brought crashing down to earth in drink, drugs, sex, and law-breaking scandals. People don't want to hear that others are doing better than they are.

My point? The same goes for work too. Nothing breeds envy and jealousy at work quite like success. So be ready to encounter increasing resistance from colleagues as you start to build your profile and gather political influence.

You will never be able to avoid the resentment entirely. But you can minimize it by prioritizing your efforts when profile-building. Respondents in the Talentspace office politics survey said that blatant self-promotion was one of their major pet hates.

So save your self-promotion for the right people. There is no point copying the entire team in on a particular email if only three or four of the recipients need to hear your news. Don't bombard others' inboxes with messages about every routine action you take.

Neither should you talk about yourself and how good you are. Talk only about your work and how it can benefit others. If you have a team working for you, try to highlight their work. Congratulate them and tell the organization when they have come up with a great idea. The Bigwigs are clever enough to realize that your team is only as good as their manager – i.e. you.

Make sure that your contributions add value. Don't monopolize meetings prattling on about minor goings-on in your team. Speak up only if you have something of genuine value to say – colleagues are remarkably adept at spotting people who are blowing only hot air. Volunteer only if you can deliver results.

Choose carefully and prioritize – it's a common theme in politicking. Focus on a few key contributions rather than many inconsequential ones. There's a fine line to be trod between being a politically savvy profile-builder and a vainglorious self-promoter. To ensure you never cross that line, give your trusted allies permission to give you a slap (either metaphorically or very literally, I don't care which) every time you stray into dangerous territory.

Champion the organizational agenda

Anne used to be a cashier supervisor at a big super-market chain. During a big change program, the management asked for volunteers to represent their departments. There wasn't any additional pay but there was a free meal involved so she signed up. At the first meeting, I remember that she was one of the most junior people there. And the most senior was her boss's boss's boss, the assistant store manager. She sounded nervous when she spoke and she didn't speak often, but when she spoke you could tell she was quite passionate about the issues she wanted to get across. Later, she noticed that the managers would now chat to her. A promotion to assistant manager and then duty manager followed in quick succession.

From an inauspicious start – Anne readily admits that volunteering sounded like it would be a "laugh" and a way to get out of being on the shop floor for a few hours – she managed to build a profile for herself.

Probably the best way to gain a profile is to keep watch for cross-departmental projects. Most organizations are in a fairly constant state of change – reorganizing, downsizing and restruc-turing seemingly at the whims of management.

But politically savvy individuals realize that standing in the way of change is a futile exercise.

Unions and union representatives often manage to slow the pace of change, but when was the last time you saw a manager promoting a union representative? Complaining about change may win over your peers, but it will mark you out as one of the old guard, a traditionalist, an old lag, and even a troublemaker among the people who matter when it comes time to decide bonuses and promotions.

Change happens whether you like it or not. Even if you privately see it as a major nuisance, look to get on board with projects that benefit the organization. They take all sorts of weird and complicated names – from work groups to change teams, project committees to task forces – but the important thing is to look for broad scopes and lofty aims. The bigger the project, the more exposure you will gain. Don't worry about not having enough clout or having the right skills. It's rare for volunteers to be turned away. What these initiatives need most are bodies who are willing to work hard – special skills aren't always required. So what's stopping you from volunteering for something right now?

Talk up the benefit

A friend of mine, a molecular biologist, was contracted by an international consumer goods company to research the comparative benefits of different skincare products. He found practically no difference between the cheap pot of moisturizer from the high street and the supposed miracle moisturizer costing twenty times as much. The only real differences were in the advertising, marketing and glossy packaging. Every time I see him he still rails at the alleged science being used to tout the latest products.

The same goes for concepts, ideas and proposals at work too. The best-packaged idea usually trumps the best idea. Positioning is often more important than actual worth. So learn to package your ideas. Translate your personal wants and needs in talk in terms of the greater organizational good – what are the benefits to the organization? Think about how your proposals could benefit the shareholders, the customers, the staff – but perhaps most importantly the managers who will implement it.

Storming into the IT manager's office and declaring, "I need a faster computer" is self-serving. But announcing "I'm worried that our slow computers mean that the sales guys aren't being able to sell as much" immediately makes it sound like a project that people should sit up and take notice of.

"The food in our canteen isn't fit for pigs and I'm sick of it" doesn't quite have the same ring to it as "Given people's increasing awareness of the need to eat healthily, maybe we should rethink our catering to appear like a caring employer."

Proposals are all about costs and benefits. But another way of pitching your ideas – apart from talking up the organizational benefits – is to play up the personal risks. By talking about what you could personally lose by getting involved in a project, it helps to reassure others that you don't have a personal agenda to push. "I could look really stupid here if this doesn't work, but I think it's worth the gamble anyway." But be careful of overdoing it. Say it once and it may sound selfless, noble. Say it twice and it will almost certainly ring false.

Deliver results

Early in my career, I had a colleague we called Golden One. He was young, charming, full of ideas and much beloved of the Bigwigs. Unfortunately for him, at the end of his first year, he hadn't hit his targets, done enough client work. Much to the annoyance of my office mate and I, Golden One still got a big fat bonus thanks to his "contributions to thought leadership" (i.e.

schmoozing and talking a good game). But in his second year it was becoming apparent that he would miss his targets for that year too. And then he left. Was he pushed or jumped? Well, let's just say that if he did jump, the bosses were no doubt watching and waving him good bye.

Golden One was superb at building relationships with Bigwigs. He always found the right words to support Bigwig initiatives without coming across to them (if not to the rest of us) as insincere. He laughed at their jokes and seemed interested in the Bigwigs as more than just colleagues – friends even. All of that stood him in good stead. Or at least it did for about 18 months. But eventually it became all too clear that he simply wasn't very good at the only part of his job that should really have mattered.

So take heed from this tale of the Golden One. Managing your reputation and raising your profile can get you very far indeed. But it has to be backed up by at least some form of tangible contribution to the business. Try to stretch your reputation too far on the basis of no results at all and you will ultimately fail.

Understand situational leverage

You have a great idea. A startling brainwave. A win–win situation for you and the business. But if your boss doesn't like it, that could be the end of the story.

Because people at work don't have to do what's best for the organization. They have their own foibles, hot buttons, personal agendas. And a good business rationale is rarely enough.

The issue could be about investing in new technology, launching a new product, hiring or firing members of the team, gaining more responsibility, getting promoted – anything. It's just that some other person – it could be your boss or any other decision maker – doesn't see the need in the same way that you do.

It's time to get dirty. To figure out how to convince them, pressurize them. It's time to think about situational leverage.

In plain English, situational leverage is the science of exercising influence in sticky situations. The people who have more leverage usually get their way. Leverage is like power, you can't see it or feel it, but it can be quantified. And people can sense it and give way to it. And I call it situational leverage because it changes from circumstance to circumstance – even with the same person you might have more leverage in one argument but less in another.

Learning to persuade other people often comes down to three simple steps that can be summarized as ACE:

- Assessing situational leverage
- Cultivating situational leverage
- Exerting situational leverage.

I'll go into the detail in the next handful of pages.

Assess situational leverage

Wielding situational leverage can be like a judo contest. When you first see opponents, you need to size them up. Then duck and dive, dodge and weave until you figure out their weak spot. A taller opponent might fall victim to a leg sweep; a shorter opponent might be a better bet for an arm-lock of some kind to pin them to the ground.

And when you come across an obstructive individual in the workplace, the first step is to size that person up, assess the leverage that you each possess in this situation. What are their strengths and weaknesses?

Someone with a grander title usually has more leverage than someone lower down the hierarchy. An individual who knows more of the key players has more leverage. Inside knowledge is a powerful source of leverage too.

Consider these other sources of leverage:

- a friendly relationship with the individual
- favors performed for the individual
- knowledge of the individual's failings, weaknesses, or secrets
- a compelling rationale that describes the benefits for the team or organization
- a good explanation as to how the particular individual would benefit personally or professionally
- the support of other people across the organization whom you can name to back you up with regard to this situation
- indirect influence on the individual from other people – particularly Bigwigs – across the organization
- being in possession of resources (e.g. time, money, people, access to information) that the other person needs – especially if the individual would have to work hard to get them elsewhere
- relationships with Bigwigs within your organization.

Of course when I say that situational leverage is

the science of getting your way, it's a rather inexact science. But at least it gives you an idea of how far you can push. The more factors you have in your favor in comparison with the other person, the more likely you are to win.

Be careful not to misjudge your leverage or that of the other party though. Overestimating your own importance and leverage could lead to a bruising car-crash encounter; underestimating your leverage could hamper unnecessarily your ability to get what you want and progress in your career. But before getting into any important debate with a colleague about whether or how to proceed with some course of action, try to assess how much leverage you and your opponent each realistically possess. An inexact science it may be, but it's better than lurching into an altercation with nothing at all.

Cultivate situational leverage

I used to wonder why some people seemed able to get away with murder while others could get no respect for anything they did. But now of course I realize that it's all to do with leverage. Have enough of it and you can do whatever you jolly well want.

Ah, but what if you judge that you actually have less situational leverage than a person you need to convince? Well if you think that it's a close call on your respective levels of leverage in that situation, you might want to give it a go – try to persuade the other person nonetheless. But the smarter alternative would be to cultivate more situational leverage first. Back away from the encounter or put it off and delay while you seek ways to bolster your leverage.

Relationships form the backbone of many leverage calculations. The more someone likes, respects, and trusts you, the more sway you will have over them. So what niceties or favors could you perform for them before your encounter? What could you do to make them more positively predisposed to you before you make your request or raise the tricky issue?

Looking back at the list of factors that can boost or undermine your level of situational leverage, think about developing the underlying rationale as to why the other person should accept your idea or proposal. What is the business case?

One of the most politically savvy tactics though, is to build credibility and support among other people across the organization. Indirect influence can be a most powerful source of situational leverage. Peer pressure is enough to make most people give way – so imagine the sway you could command if you manage to sign up Bigwigs to your side too.

In enlisting the support of others, be sure to approach a broad spectrum of people. It's natural to want to approach the people you know first; the people you know will be receptive to your ideas. But by approaching only the people you know, you could get blindsided, thinking you have plenty of support when the other person might have more. If you really want to gather heavy-duty support, try to reach out to the hard-to-get people and convince them to come on board.

Like I said, situational leverage is an inexact science. But the key to it is simple – more of it is better.

Exert situational leverage

Exerting situational leverage is like a game of poker. The person who shows their cards first puts themselves in the weaker position.

Jessica, an account manager, complains that one of her fellow account managers has been asking her to do "small" work favors for him – ranging from crunching numbers to filling in for him at meetings. And she has had little choice but to comply. Because he is the account management team's representative on a special project group. A group that will ultimately decide who gets to travel to Shanghai to open their new office next year. Unfortunately for Jessica, she has shown all her cards, made her desperation to work in the new office all too clear, and opened herself up to sly manipulation.

The other account manager is no more senior than Jessica. But his current position gives him plenty of situational leverage. Short of demanding sexual favors, he can ask for just about anything.

Of course most situations are not quite so one-sided. If you had so much more situational leverage you wouldn't need to calculate and plan the best way to get your way. You could just barge into someone's office and make your demands.

In reality, you need to play the game of situational leverage just as you would poker. Decide on the other person's likely tactics and decide how to play your hand. See if you can expose their point of view and the sources of leverage they possess.

Share gradually your reasons why the other person should come round to your way of thinking. Consider each of the factors that contributes to your situational leverage, and think of the best way of sharing them with the other person. For example, just because you may have various Bigwigs signed up to support your idea or proposal doesn't mean that you should immediately blurt that out. If you have a compelling business argument, then that should probably come out before you try to pull in the personal favors.

Of course, you could try outright bluffing too. Claim to have sources of leverage that you don't quite actually have. The perception of having leverage could trump the reality of having none. But it's a risky strategy. And how good exactly is your poker face?

Choose leverage points

One of my clients, Helene, is Vice President of Human Capital for Europe at a marketing communications firm. Because she does not sit on the management team, she is frequently frustrated by the discussions and decisions that go on behind closed doors. But rather than spreading herself too thinly in trying to persuade six vice presidents separately, she focuses her efforts. She identifies the VP who seems the most aligned with any of her proposals. And she spends time with that one, explaining the rationale, answering questions, turning meetings into brainstorming sessions and ensuring the VP is personally invested in the proposal. It works pretty well for her.

The principle of situational leverage still works

when you are trying to persuade a group of people. It just gets more complicated. Helene loses a chunk of situational leverage because of her rank – she hasn't been invited to sit on the management team. But she makes up for it to a degree by creating an advocate who can argue on her behalf. By choosing carefully and directing her attention on one rather than many, she creates a leverage point that often sees her proposals being voted through more often than if she had tried to influence all six of the VPs.

Never underestimate the power of personal relationships. Often, the investment of time in one robust relationship counts for more than trying to influence too many people at a time. Find the right personal and professional buttons to push to get the right person on side. A single person who is committed to the same agenda will carry more weight than an army of people who are vaguely inclined.

Be careful of influencing too many people at once for another reason too. People talk when they get together. No one likes to feel that they have been manipulated so if you are using tactics that could in any way be interpreted as under-hand, you could be in trouble. And trouble is never good.

Create credibility chains

People rarely do what is right or fair, I think we're agreed on that. But everyone listens to someone else. If you can't influence someone, work out who can.

James, a senior underwriter with a large insurance company, had an idea for reducing costs in handling a certain type of claim. Unfortunately, his manager, let's call him Manager A, thought that the project was too time-consuming to merit further consideration. Without sufficient situational leverage, James could easily have let the idea die. But he seeded the idea with an underwriter in an unrelated department to share with his boss, Manager B. When Manager B told his peers that he was pursuing a new idea for reducing costs, Manager A jumped on the bandwagon, enlarging the scope of the project to transcend departmental divisions. And James got invited to represent the views of their team.

Without necessarily understanding it, James had created a credibility chain to influence his boss. Each person in the chain had enough credibility to influence the next person in the chain.

Using credibility chains is the logical extension of understanding the network of relationships around you and looking for leverage points. Even though you might not have enough sway with a key player does not mean you cannot influence someone who does have the sway you need.

But don't expect a quick fix. It takes time to convince the first person in the chain to come round to your way of thinking, let alone getting them to speak to the next person in the chain. And at each stage you need to understand the hot buttons of the next person in the chain. Work out what their professional and personal needs are and coach the person with whom you do have contact on how they might best position the idea to convince the next person in the chain.

Your influence will weaken as the chain gets longer. And the chain's power to influence is only as strong as its weakest link. But with patience and planning, creating credibility chains could allow you a far wider span of influence than you might think. Be patient. Start planning.

Turn networks into coalitions

Your network should be an almost random group of people – diversity giving you access to sources of information that an overly uniform network cannot. Within your network, each individual has their own hot buttons, their personal and professional agendas. Many of them will not know each other; some might not get on with each other. The only thing they really have in common is that they all know you. And while they can act as your eyes and ears, they rarely have any collective power.

But find a couple of people with similar personal or professional agendas and suddenly you have a coalition, a cluster of like-minded individuals. Even if they only have momentarily coinciding goals, that might just be good enough.

Say the HR director doesn't want to see a particular internal candidate, John, promoted into the sales director's role because she worries that he doesn't have the right skills. Perhaps the finance director simply doesn't get on with John, believing him to be too independent-minded to kowtow to the finance director. Lo and behold, you have a coalition. The HR and finance directors may have little else in common. They might even clash more of the time than they get on. But in this one particular instance, they may be united in a common goal.

Suppose they could find another person to join the coalition. Perhaps one of the other internal candidates for the role. The strength of the coalition quickly grows. Poor John doesn't stand a chance. And once the deed is done the HR and finance directors can go back to arguing among themselves again.

Coalitions have a strength that exceeds the sum of their parts. They can agree on plans of attack. They can decide collectively to voice their concerns, pressurize key individuals, focus on key leverage points.

It makes sense to look for like-minded individuals. To build coalitions to support your own goals. For any decision, seek supporters who might side with you. Even if you usually have little to do with them, even if you have no respect for them. The fact that you have a momentarily overlapping purpose should be enough to encourage you to side with them. Why make life harder for yourself when there may be co-conspirators out there to support your cause?

Issue invitations, not orders

Marketing executive Alex left a technology business to take on a bigger role in a service company. To his dismay, he discovered that staff rarely knew what was going in other divisions, leading to duplicated efforts and huge inefficiencies. His boss said that the issue was nothing to do with their department. And his boss's boss said that there weren't the resources to tackle it. Out of desperation, Alex gathered together a group of colleagues from across departments and divisions who also felt disgruntled by the company's lackadaisical communications.

Fast-forward to the present day and colleagues from across the company can access a wealth of information on their intranet about product launches, previous applications to tender for different clients, and a lively "FAQ You" frequently asked questions board. He had succeeded. Alex managed to pull off something not far short of a miracle, creating a company-wide intranet with almost no resources and a team cobbled together out of peeved volunteers.

So invite others to join you when you want to pursue a goal. Allow it to become their goal too.

People hate being told what to do. They don't like to be told that something is good for them or the organization. It's a *fait accompli* to tell them you know better than they do. But they love to feel involved.

Rally support for your cause by approaching people with your raw ideas. Seek their input; invite them to weigh up the pros and cons. Allow them to feel that the idea belongs as much to them as it does to you. Encourage them to invest time and energy in fleshing an idea out, formalizing it, and turning it into a fully fledged business case. If you allow them to participate, they will feel emotionally invested in your idea. The more emotionally invested they feel about it, the more they will want to evangelize about it to others and get them involved too.

Some would-be political players hold on to ideas, believing that ideas give them power. And ideas do have a power. But they are most powerful when others can see you turning your ideas into practical initiatives that benefit the organization. So share freely and invite others to join you in striving for those goals. Ask questions to gain support, don't preach.

Pay attention to non-verbal leakage

The first time a client told me how unhappy she was with my work, I didn't actually realize how lucky I was. We'd been working together for nearly a year when she told me that my attention to detail had slipped dramatically of late and that I had used "inappropriate humor" in a recent meeting.

I was stunned and went away deeply miserable.

But in retrospect I realize that I was lucky because she could have chosen instead to cancel the contract and find a new consultant to work with. The fact that she had confronted the issue turned out to be good news for me and we carried on working together.

Now this may sound strange, but it's actually

good news when someone tells you how hacked off with you they are. If they get angry or upset with you, it may be a bit unpleasant and take you aback, but you should be pleased.

Because when they tell you what they are thinking or feeling, you can take that away and work on it. You can try to come up with counter-arguments or think about ways of overcoming their objections or behaving differently.

Most people fall into one of two categories. Some people are more than happy to assert themselves. Okay, they may occasionally speak their mind a little too assertively – crossing the line into becoming aggressive. But that's still fine because at least they are telling you what they think.

It's the silent ones who are more often deadly. These other types may back down, capitulate, stay quiet, and refuse to impart what they really think or feel. Perhaps because they hate conflict, they may nod in mute agreement with you. But they will be shooting invisible daggers at you. They may seem to support you in public but seek ways to undermine or sabotage you behind your back.

So learn to read others' body language. If they suddenly shy away from making eye contact or become a little too quiet, tread carefully. If they agree with you too quickly, be cautious. If some-one looks unhappy, they probably are. And it's up to you to make them happy again.

Be incredibly sensitive about it though. Perhaps catch them on their own and away from the prying eyes and ears of others. Tell them you sense they may not be 100 percent convinced or happy. But speak the unspoken and make sure they tell you what they really think. And if they start shouting and screaming at you about how much they hate you or disagree with your ideas, then count yourself lucky.

Focus your energies

Hands up if it annoys you that some people get away with murder at work. My hand is up. Personally, I can't stand people who shirk responsibility, spend hours gossiping rather than working, surfing the net, chatting, producing no results.

In particular, a colleague of mine used to have the nickname "Teflon hands." He had the most amazing ability to shrug off work. Which used to irritate the hell out of me.

But grumbling about such individuals is pointless. Yes, voicing your disapproval might endear you to a few of your colleagues. To other grumblers and whiners. But not the people who count.

You might be tempted to intervene too.

Perhaps have words with them about putting in a bit more effort or report them to someone. And while it might have some short-term benefit to the overall team (and be immensely person-ally satisfying), the more important question is whether doing so would help you to achieve your personal career goals.

Many organizations pay only lip service to coaching and developing their staff. In reality, they couldn't be less bothered. The Bigwigs will probably just see your efforts to intervene in someone else's work as pointless meddling and interference. Kicking up a fuss and drawing attention to yourself for all the wrong reasons.

While it probably hurts your sense of fairness that others get away with so little work, think carefully about wasting your energies on them. Focus instead on removing yourself from the situation. If you don't like your colleagues, don't bitch about their laziness or stab them in the back. Try to get a transfer to another team. Rather than trying to bring them up to scratch, try to get yourself promoted away from their mediocrity. Don't waste breath carping about them or trying to turn them around. Concen-trate on your own career rather than theirs. Some people will never change; so just leave them to it.

Swallow your pride

Elton John (or Elton John and boy band Blue – if you are one of the younger generation) sang that sorry seems to be the hardest word. And it's true. Most of us are terrible at apologizing.

But becoming politically savvy isn't only about building relationships. It's also about using your brain.

The whole point of identifying career goals and devising a grand plan is that you can make decisions about how to invest your time and effort. In particular, it helps you to remember when to back down. To lose the fight in order to win the eventual war.

For those important decisions, we've already discussed how to assess leverage points and marshal enough situational leverage to get your way. But for other, less important decisions, learn to back down. Even if you are clearly in the right and the other person is in the wrong. Even if you have written confirmation, sworn witnesses and signed affidavits on your side. Because while it may be satisfying to prove your point, consider which is more important to you – proving a point by arguing until you have ground the other person's self-esteem into the ground and destroyed the relationship or backing down and retaining the relationship?

Think about it. You probably know people at

work who try to argue that white is black and black is white. Even if you have insurmountable evidence, show them convincing proof, they never back down. Even worse, they never apologize or accept that you might have been right. And because they argue the point with everything, you just can't tell when to bother listening anymore.

We all hate to fail, back down, lose face. But be prepared to do it. Be ready to concede, give way, lose arguments, and even admit that you were wrong. And do it graciously and wholeheartedly, not grudgingly between gritted teeth.

Swallow your pride because it's more important to be credible and to repair long-term relationships than to be proved right. After all, have you ever heard anyone comment: "He's unsuccessful but, hey, at least he's still got his pride?"

Seek criticism, not praise

Okay, I confess. This is a tough one for me. I'd much rather hear praise than criticism. But let me explain.

Of course it's a great feeling when things go right. Hurrah. But it's easy to get compliments if you are on the lookout for them. When you go about seeking praise, you will find it.

So when you have handed in a piece of work or completed a successful project, ask what was wrong with it. Especially ask for it when you feel proud of it. If they tell you that it was okay, fine or good, persist and ask for constructive criticism. Even if they continue to reassure you that it's excellent, great, or fantastic – keep digging.

You may not like what you hear, but at least you'll know. You can take action, make sure you don't make even the tiniest of mistakes the next time around. Forewarned is forearmed and all that.

Asking for criticism shows how humble you are. You pre-empt others from resenting you and your achievements. By getting the chance to comment on what wasn't quite right about your work, it makes them feel a bit better about themselves. Rather than resenting you, they become proud that they have helped to shape and develop you. When you succeed, they can pat themselves on the back and believe that it was their words of wisdom that set you on the right path.

Because the old adage that "pride comes before a fall" has scuppered the career of more than one would-be office politician. Believe your own hype and you'll soon overextend your reach. You will believe that you have more leverage than you actually possess and be brought down to earth. Very hard. And very suddenly. So ask: What could be better?

Celebrate in silence

Picture the scene. The valiant hero, a secret agent, has been caught by the evil genius. The villain can't resist but to show off his brilliance so gloats and shares his evil plan for world domination. What happens next? Of course the hero escapes, pushing the villain into his own shark-infested pool or into the path of the oncoming laser beam, and foils the evil plot. Cut to the hero kissing the girl as the end credits roll.

No one likes boasting. So even when you achieve your political goals, learn to celebrate in silence. Don't blow it all by revealing that you had a grand plan for getting that promotion or that transfer, for heading up your own division or getting a mammoth pay rise. Sharing the details of your plan makes it sound too deliberate, too manipulative, scheming.

Be politically active. But never be so obvious that you are labeled "political." Remember that most people hate politics. They don't understand that politicking is only a means to an end, and that the means doesn't automatically have to be underhand. Confide your winning plans to even one person who tells only their closest friend ... Before you know it everyone knows. And they feel used, jealous, unhappy.

Sure, go celebrate your success with family or close friends. But resist the siren call to draw attention to your success back in the office. No one likes a braggart so compose yourself and try to exhibit your continuing humility at work. Whatever you do, make sure to avoid the mistake that all evil villains intent on world domination ultimately commit.

Work around your boss

Your boss will be responsible for the very best and worst moments of your working life. You will at times feel constrained, frustrated, or angered by your boss's decisions. Whether you get interesting work or a rough ride is up to your boss. And the big decisions – getting that pay rise, promotion, or transfer to the office in the Bahamas – rest greatly on the shoulders of your boss too. It makes sense to manage your manager.

Managing your boss effectively doesn't mean trying to remove them by political means. No, they have too much leverage and it would be foolish to try. However, you can try to understand their personality, their working style, and the unique pressures they face. And then figure out how to work around their foibles, strengths and weaknesses.

Start by learning about their particular pressures. What are their goals and targets? If you understand what they are trying to achieve – both professionally and personally – you have a hope of focusing on the right projects, tasks, and pieces of work that will get you remembered for all the right reasons.

Then consider their working style. For example, while some managers communicate their expectations clearly and at great length, many do not. Which doesn't mean that they don't have expectations – just that they aren't very good at telling you explicitly what they want or need from you. And if things go wrong guess who will get the blame? Not your boss certainly. So make sure you go to lengths to discover exactly what needs doing.

Consider how they like to take in information. Blackberry, paper, phone, or face-to-face? Some bosses like to receive information in written form that they can mull over at their own pace. Or if yours prefers to talk issues through and ask questions in person – do they prefer team meetings or one-to-ones? Formal meetings with set agendas or informal get-togethers? And is once a week too much or twice a day too little?

Decision making is another area of frequent tension. While some bosses need to feel involved and like to be consulted, others prefer to delegate and hate to be bothered.

In many ways, managing a boss is little different to adapting to the styles of your other colleagues. It's just that a boss has so much more sway over your working life. Your boss is too big a part of your working life not to make a supreme effort in accommodating them and doing things their way.

Deal with a toxic boss

A respondent in the Talentspace office politics survey described her boss as subscribing to the "mushroom" school of management – "He kept us in the dark and fed us shit."

A person in your position shouldn't have to put up with a toxic boss. But there's not a lot you can do to manage one. Some so-called experts talk about the importance of having a transparent and open dialogue with your boss. Of communicating your unhappiness with their decisions or leadership style and trying to rectify the situation. Sure you could try to have a constructive discussion, but it's the kind of naive behavior that a purist would indulge in. Pick the wrong type of boss to talk to and it could amount to political suicide.

Few bosses respond well to negative feedback.

Tell them that you weren't pleased with some-thing or that they could have done something more effectively – even in the most constructive tones – and you will damage their pride. Like a slap in the face or a poke in the eye with a sharp stick, it will hurt their self-image of themselves as good leaders.

Your tools in managing a toxic boss are fairly limited. While your boss can use both carrot and stick to reward and punish you, you can use only the carrot. You don't have the leverage to punish their bad behaviors, only to use positive strokes to encourage their good ones. Treat them as big babies and lavish praise on them when they behave well. It's not half as effective as being able to chastise them when they are naughty, but it's the best that you have.

Truly toxic bosses are a nightmare. You can maneuver around a difficult colleague, but not your boss. I'm afraid there really isn't that much you can do. Unless your boss is commonly regarded by the Bigwigs as a bit of a liability, you're stuck with the situation. So the politically savvy individual will focus not on trying to change the boss but on devising an escape plan – a promotion, a transfer to another department, a new job. What are your options?

Be a pragmatic leader

There's a story going around about an employee who decided to exact her revenge on her toxic boss by adding laxative to his coffee while simultaneously getting his car towed away so that he wouldn't be able to drive home.

Whether it's a retelling of actual events or just a modern myth, we'll never know – I leave it to you to decide. But what is true is that more than a handful of respondents in the Talentspace politics survey said that they had issues with their bosses. They admitted to acts of revenge ranging from "accidentally" removing their boss from key distribution lists to spreading (untrue) rumors that a boss had paid for an adult movie in their hotel room and claimed it back as a business expense. And those are just the ones that people happily admit to – so who knows what else is going on that employees are keeping quiet about?

Unfortunately this is all rather bad news if you happen to manage any sort of team. Even if you think of yourself as a great manager. Are you 100 percent certain that you are doing the very best job you can?

There are many tomes written on how to transform yourself into a great leader. They usually blather on about setting visions and inspiring others to great deeds. Which is all fine if you are the chief exec and are trying to squeeze that extra bit of effort out of the people who all work for you. But the politically savvy person knows better than to waste too much time on all of that.

If your goal is to get promoted, then the reality is that you will be leaving your team behind soon. So don't expend all of your energies trying to turn them all into superstars. Don't invest too much of your time trying to coach, nurture, and develop your team. The politically minded individual is pragmatic, understanding that the love and adoration of your team means almost nothing when it comes to climbing the organizational tree.

Of course the hatred and loathing of your team can set you back enormously. But so long as your team at least tolerates and accepts you, that should be enough for the politically savvy leader.

Create rules – and stick by them

In a fantasyland, you as a manager would be able to assign fun and challenging tasks to everyone. But back in the real world of organizational life, your team will have to handle not only the exciting and fun tasks but also some mediocre or downright unpleasant duties too.

You can't be expected to wave a magic wand and make the boring or disagreeable work go away. But what you can do is to establish clear rules about what needs doing.

What is the task and when does it need completing? Who should do it? How should it get done? And what are the rewards or consequences of doing it well or badly?

Team members hate uncertainty and ambiguity. And while laying down explicit rules will never turn you into an inspirational leader, it will at least earn you the grudging respect of your team.

But remember that people hate being told what to do without understanding why they are doing it. The most important question isn't about what, who, when or how – but why. "Clear your desks at the end of the day" sounds petty and controlling. But "Clear your desks at the end of the day because a corporate spy once stole confidential documents" presents a clear rationale that is more likely to be followed.

Because. It's a simple word. But terribly effective.

Always explain when issuing instructions and delegating work. And listen to your own explanations. If your reason doesn't sound compelling to yourself, then it probably isn't. So don't ask others to do what you wouldn't do.

Finally, remember that while it's your team's job to do what you tell them, they don't have to do it well. They can choose to be difficult and obstructive or responsible and helpful. If you want to unlock that extra discretionary effort that is theirs to give, then make sure you thank them and show your genuine appreciation for their hard work. The key word here is genuine. But if you can't be genuine, at least act as if you mean it every time.

Be totally ruthless

The word "ruthless" summons up images of a cigar-smoking business mogul rubbing his hands together in glee as he watches his competitor's factory go down in flames. Of the cruel boss firing his loyal secretary on the day before Christmas just to save a few dollars.

And indeed the would-be office politician needs to be ceaselessly ruthless. Ruthless to the point of making it an art form. But ruthless only in how you manage your time.

A key principle of becoming politically savvy is to realize that not all people and all actions are of equal worth. Yes, yes, it's neither right nor fair. It's just the way of the world and all that. But if some people, tasks and situations are more important, then you need to choose ruthlessly how to spend your precious time.

Ruthlessness does not equate to rudeness. You may not want to spend hours chatting to the receptionist or the sandwich guy. But neither do you need to belittle or ignore them. It's the kind of attitude that sparks revolutions and triggers uprisings. And you wouldn't want that, would you?

Be ruthless in prioritizing your time with people. Prune relationships that drain you of time and energy in order to cultivate more fruitful ones. Be brutal in choosing projects. Cull activities that don't get you noticed.

Finance departments calculate the cost–benefit ratio of investment decisions and business plans. So take a similar mindset. What gains do you hope to achieve by choosing to work on one particular project rather than another? Who should you spend time having a drink with after work? Should you spend your lunch hour poring over last month's figures or chatting over a sandwich with your boss?

Or your diary is packed with meetings. Too many dull, meaningless meetings with lackeys and cronies to allow you to focus on what matters. But what's stopping you from skipping a meeting? Making an excuse, giving a reason to slip away. If there are better ways to spend your time, prioritize, do what you need to do. Take a few minutes before you get to work every day to decide how you're going to spend your time – identify the people you need to speak to, the maneuvers you need to perform.

Too often we lapse into doing what comes easily rather than what would benefit our careers most. It's human nature to be lazy sometimes. But the canny office politician can't afford to be lazy, to lie back, take it easy. Of course it's your prerogative to pursue what you want to do rather than what you need to do. But what you want to do may not further your career as much as what you need to do. Take it easy or get ahead – the choice is yours.

CONFRONTING ADVERSARIES

In work, as in life, people are often both our greatest source of grief and joy. And boy can some of the people at work cause us grief. There are some nasty, venomous, unsavory characters in the workplace. There are some incompetent, oblivious, hopeless ones too.

I define an adversary as anyone who gets in your way, impedes your progress, or stops you from reaching your goals. And this last part of the book looks at how to tackle them.

Respondents in the Talentspace politics survey sent in dozens and dozens of stories of destructive politicking. There were tales of colleagues unfairly blaming others, spreading malicious rumors, and casting aspersions. Co-workers were said to have fabricated data, failed to pass important information on, and manipulated circumstances to suit themselves. There were stories of teammates who made promises and never delivered, or who said one thing to your face but then said the opposite behind your back. Then there were reports of adversaries who were only too happy to use tactics such as verbal abuse, unfair criticism, thinly veiled threats, and cold-shouldering. The list goes on. And I'm sure it probably sounds all too familiar to you too.

But there's also a different kind of adversary, ones who are not intentionally malicious but merely incompetent. They may be rubbish managers, terrible at their job, useless at pretty much everything. Human and very fallible, they may be ineffectual and unaware of their own ineptitude. But just because they can't help it and don't realize it doesn't mean that they can't still have a devastating effect on your career.

Thankfully adversaries are actually quite rare. Yes, some of your colleagues may not be terribly supportive or helpful. But it's less because they are out to undermine you than the fact they are merely indifferent to you and can't be bothered to help. They may not like you, but they don't hate you either. Only a very few people will set out deliberately to undercut you or harm your career. The danger of seeing too many enemies around you is that you create a self-fulfilling prophecy – turning colleagues from being merely unsympathetic towards you to disliking or even loathing you if you start to treat them as enemies.

Only occasionally should you be unlucky enough to encounter a real adversary. When it happens, it's no good hoping they will go away, because they won't. You are the only one with the power to deal with it, no one else. So let's talk about dealing with adversaries.

Identify the shapes and forms of political attack

Political attacks such as threats and overtly harmful behavior are only too easy to spot. But people are usually too clever to engage in openly damaging activities, so most political attacks are much more subtle and underhand.

A few years ago I coached a sales manager who told me how managers would send group emails to share good news about new contracts they had won – heaping glory on themselves. One manager, let's call him John, was significantly behind on his targets, but when he did secure a major deal, a fellow manager sent out an email congratulating him. On the face of it, it seemed as if the colleague was celebrating John's success. But it also served to remind senior management that John was still underperforming by some margin. John departed the business at the end of the year and his existing clients were redistributed to the other sales managers.

Politicking could come in the guise of a joke with a mostly humorous but perhaps slightly hurtful edge, raising the faintest of doubts about your competence. A colleague might offer to help you with your workload in front of the boss, making an implicit statement that you are not fit to deal with it all yourself. Or a teammate might raise a recent failure of yours in a meeting under the pretext of wanting to learn the lessons, all the while hammering that knife further into your back.

Inaction can be as harmful as action too. Is anyone forgetting to pass important messages on to you – perhaps just a little too often? Are key decisions being made without your input? Is a colleague neglecting to include you in activities or a manager failing to offer you training or other opportunities?

Politicking comes in many shapes and forms. So question the motives of all that goes on around you. If something feels suspicious, then pay more attention the next time it happens. If something seems too good to be true, then it usually is. I am not advocating that you should be paranoid and immediately suspicious of all of your colleagues' motives. But a second or two of thought to think about the reasons someone is behaving in a certain manner could save you much angst and later pain. Whenever you see someone behaving differently, ask yourself "why?"

Concentrate on the adversaries who count

My first employer recruited a dozen junior consultants at the same time every year. In my intake, there was one junior consultant who just didn't like me at all. Maybe I said or did something inadvertently that upset him. Perhaps it was because I hadn't attended the right sort of school or university. Whatever it was, it troubled me and I went out of my way to be nice to him. I wanted to be liked.

But in retrospect I realize that I was wasting my time. Because he wasn't important. Yes, of course I wanted to be liked. But he wasn't important in career terms because he was a junior consultant. I now realize that I spent too much of my time trying to befriend him. When I could have been spending so much more of my energies on impressing the Bigwigs who decided on matters like promotion and annual bonuses.

In your working life, there are going to be people you don't see eye-to-eye with. Perhaps because of your different backgrounds, personalities, senses of humor, or some imagined offence or a real slight. And of course these unsatisfactory relationships may range from being somewhat stressful to incredibly distressing for you. But if you wish to develop your political savvy and achieve your career goals, the most important question you must learn to ask yourself is whether the relationship is of sufficient importance to be worth fixing.

Some of the more naive so-called experts out there talk about the importance of trying to develop harmonious relationships with everyone. Not true, I say. Given the reality of your limited time and patience, you may need to live with some relationships that are less than perfect.

On the other hand, don't assume that you can snub people purely because you are senior to them.

Before joining Talentspace I worked in an organization in which one of the members of the team again took a dislike to me. (Honestly, it doesn't happen often though!) She wasn't my boss. Neither was she a peer. In fact she was a member of the support staff team. But she was still very important because she was charming and immensely popular with the Bigwigs. While the formal hierarchy should have meant that I could merely ignore her, the political reality was that I had to make efforts to mend the relationship and limit the damage she could do to my career.

Apply the same level of ruthless consideration in deciding which unproductive relationships to tackle as you do in deciding whom to build significant relationships with.

Separate intention from action

If you feel someone is out to damage you, avoid blundering into a confrontation with them. Your very first step should be a step back. Step back from the situation and observe. Seek the reasons behind your adversary's behavior. Are they using such tactics deliberately and intentionally to undermine you? Or are they merely blundering idiots, oblivious to the impact that their behavior is having on you?

The law talks about *actus reus* – the physical act of a crime or wrongful behavior. However, for a successful conviction, there also has to be *mens rea* – criminal intent or the knowledge that they are doing wrong. So when someone seems to be out to harm you, take the time to separate intention from action.

For example, your adversary might genuinely not realize that speaking up in a meeting effectively points the finger of blame at you. Maybe they don't appreciate how offensive they can sound or how hurtful they can be by leaving you out of important activities. So don't automatically assume the worst. What might at first seem to be malicious behavior could turn out to be mere incompetence or thoughtless behavior. Stupidity is a very different offence to the crime of conniving nastiness.

Dealing with a deliberate attack on you may require a carefully considered plan of action. But dealing with incompetence or a lack of thought may require only a few words spoken gently to the person in private. But note the key words in that sentence. Gently. And in private.

Delve further into an adversary's intentions

Company X is a retail bank in which only one in 20 branch managers can be promoted up to area manager. As you can imagine, the branch managers take every opportunity to talk up their own brilliance to senior managers and knife colleagues in the back. But political maneuvering is part and parcel of the bank's structure and culture and, for the most part, the branch managers understand that it is a vital part of getting ahead.

Contrast that with Paul's situation. Within a respectable law firm, Paul was an associate – a junior lawyer. But he felt that he was being picked on by one of the senior secretaries who had been with the firm for over 25 years. She always used to deal with his work last and, on more than one occasion, snubbed his attempts to build even a modicum of rapport with her.

Now the secretary had no political motivation to get ahead. She wasn't looking for promotion. She picked on Paul merely because she seemed to enjoy it and could get away with it.

Sometimes colleagues go on the offensive not for professional and career reasons – but for personal reasons. They do it for no other reason than because putting others down makes them feel good.

But the important thing to realize about being bullied is that you are not at fault. Even though a bully may have singled you out, it is not because you are not good enough. In fact, the opposite is often true. Targets of harassment and intimidation are often above average in popularity, competence and diligence. The fact that you are good is often enough to bring on feelings of envy in the bully.

Such adversaries are psychologically flawed. They have a deep-seated need to exploit other people in order to address their own insecurities. While most people try to better themselves in order to feel good, insecure adversaries resort to doing others down to achieve the same goal. They want the life you have. But because they can't seem to get it, they take it out on you.

They can't be reasoned with. They aren't out to damage your reputation and career in order to get ahead. They do it merely out of spite and malice. It's not about political gain but personal pleasure. So understand that, unless you take action, the bullying is unlikely to stop.

Understand the enemy

Adversaries come in different guises. Remember that even if their actions are damaging, there may not always be a malicious intent. And even when there is a deliberately evil intent, it can stem from different reasons.

In fact, adversaries tend to fall into four broad categories and it's up to you to figure out where each particular one stands:

- *Inadvertent adversaries* – people who are simply incompetent and/or unaware of their impact on others. If you manage to tell them how you feel, they will usually respond with surprise at how you feel and be ready to make amends.
- *Insecure adversaries* – these bullies have psychological issues of their own and need to put others down to feel good about themselves.
- *Revenge-motivated adversaries* – these adversaries are out to damage you because

they feel you have wronged them in some way. Either for a real or imagined grievance, these adversaries believe they are merely taking justifiable actions to defend themselves against your behavior!

- *Politically motivated adversaries* – these adversaries will lie, cheat, backstab, and deceive because they see you as an obstacle who needs to be removed for them to succeed in achieving their own goals.

The bad news is that tackling any adversary will ultimately mean confronting them, talking to them, hammering out a solution. But before you do that, consider some of the further steps you need to take to arm yourself fully for the confrontation.

Choose your moment

As the joke goes, just because you're paranoid doesn't mean they aren't out to get you. But sometimes it's worth biding your time rather than leaping into the fray of combat.

Let's say it's that time of year when discretionary bonuses are about to be awarded. In a team meeting, a colleague makes a slightly critical remark about you. But is it just a thoughtless comment or the start of a pernicious campaign to destroy your credibility?

Of course you can't tell. At least, not yet.

The following week, she makes another cutting observation about you. And then you hear from a trusted source that she's done it again – and this time behind your back. Okay, there's a pattern emerging. She's definitely out to get you. But is she motivated by political gain – perhaps trying to put you down to get a bigger bonus? Or does she think that you recently harmed her in some way and is now out for revenge? You still can't be certain about her motives.

Then a couple of days later you overhear her losing her temper with a customer. And then she makes a snide comment to the boss as well. Hmm. So maybe there is no threat after all. Perhaps stress is causing her to behave erratically. The poor woman is not so much deliberately maneuvering as an inadvertent adversary.

And so with any potential adversary's actions, wait until you can get a better idea of what is going on. Acting on the basis of only one or two incidents could lead you to the wrong conclusions. Learn to be patient. Hold back until you are certain.

On the other hand, don't let that be an excuse to procrastinate either. Once when I wasn't getting on with a particular colleague, I tried to bury the issue. Pretend that it didn't matter. Hope that it might go away. But problems don't just go away on their own. Praying that it will sort itself out doesn't tackle the problem, it merely prolongs it. Like having a bad toothache, you can try to put up with the agony or you can take action and visit the dentist. Don't allow yourself to tolerate difficult people. If it's important, bide your time only until you are certain action needs to be taken. Then take it.

Collect evidence

In the world of advertising, Harry and Paul have charmed dozens of clients into giving them millions of pounds of business. Harry was Chairman and majority shareholder of the firm; Paul was one of five board directors. Unfortunately neither could stand the other and their relationship ranged from mildly competitive to openly aggressive.

About a year ago, Paul suddenly stopped delivering on his sales targets. Harry asked Paul to leave. Paul demanded a pay off in order to leave. Eventually Harry fired Paul – accusing him of stealing clients. But while everyone suspected that Paul was preparing to set up a rival firm, no one could confirm it. Paul countered by filing a claim for unfair dismissal and it looks almost certain that Harry will have to pay Paul a crippling amount of compensation.

Confrontation is always an ugly business – but never more so than if you blunder into it without enough evidence. Emotions run high and can easily lead to irrational decisions with possibly costly consequences.

So get your facts straight. A police detective would never confront an alleged criminal without the evidence to secure a conviction, and neither should you. Document incidents. Look for physical evidence, save emails, hoard letters.

Even when there is no physical evidence, just make a note in a diary. Don't rely on your memory. Human memory is fallible. Now you may think that you will be able to remember all of the details. But under the accusing gaze and wilting questioning of opposing counsel, are you completely certain that you will be able to recall every single detail and nuance without tripping up even once? Keep track of who was involved, when it happened, what was said.

You must be able to describe events in sufficient detail. You might need to cite examples in a private one-to-one discussion with your adversary. Or if events take a turn for the worse, you might well end up in front of an industrial tribunal and a grilling from legal professionals. So make sure that you get your facts as clear and consistent as possible. Trust me. This one's important.

Get a second opinion

You're under attack. Of course you're unhappy. Perhaps you feel at times helpless and resigned or furious and determined to exact revenge. But emotions can blunt our ability to think clearly and choose the best course of action. We can act on impulse, blow our best chance, and regret it later. So take a step back and seek a second opinion from someone you trust.

Avoid confiding only in close friends whose gut feeling may be to take your side automatically. Of course friends should want to support you. But what you need at this moment is clarity and objectivity, not tea and sympathy.

The key here is to find someone whose judgment you trust. Someone who can ask you the tough questions, who can look beyond how you feel to the facts at the heart of the problem. You might not know them that well at work, but what you need is objectivity rather than support at this moment in time. Perhaps it might be a colleague in another department whom you trust. Or maybe an ex-colleague who has left the organization but who still knows some of the players. Look for anyone who can offer you the objectivity to see both sides of the situation.

Approach such an individual and ask for their time. Explain that you rate their judgment and would like an independent perspective on a problem of yours. Assure them you are looking not for sympathy but an impartial view on the situation.

Talk them through the evidence you have collected and ask their opinion. Talk them through the options you have considered. What would they do in your situation?

A good second opinion should raise questions that you might not have considered yourself. A good second opinion might advise you to collect further evidence or try new tactics you have yet to consider. But in seeking a second opinion, be wary of confiding too widely. Talk only to those people you are sure you can trust. Remember that canny office politicians offering a sympathetic ear may have hidden agendas of their own. And your admissions might be just what they need to stab you in the back.

Consider that revenge is sweet

In evaluating the reasons behind attacks on you, most people are quick to point the finger at either politically motivated reasons or personal insecurities on the part of a persistent bully.

But there is always the possibility that you may be at least partly to blame for the situation. Yes, your adversary may be leaving you out of key communications and making overly critical remarks during meetings. Perhaps they have singled you out, shouted at you, or even made threatening comments. But it can happen that adversaries sometimes believe that they are the ones who have been wronged. That you started it all and that their behavior is merely a justifiable defense against your transgressions.

A tiny bit of scientific study here. Apparently people can get into a "spiral of incivility" without even realizing it. Two eminent researchers by the names of Blau and Andersson report that people can get into a pattern of mutually destructive behavior with possibly quite innocent beginnings. Perhaps one person makes a joke that is misunderstood and taken a little more personally than was intended. Maybe someone is too busy to respond to a request for help or makes a decision that isn't entirely favorable. In turn, this initial action could lead to slightly less polite behavior from the other person, which in turn provokes still more discourteous responses. And so it escalates and spirals out of control.

Revenge-motivated adversaries believe that you started it all. Which you might find surprising and difficult to believe. When I coach individuals, their immediate response is always to blame the other person. But they say that it takes two to tango and it's sometimes true that you may be at least somewhat, or (possibly) even mostly, to blame for the situation.

Neither of you may remember the initial trigger. Perhaps even a single word or inadvertent look. But if the relationship is important enough and you need to salvage it, who do you think must take the responsibility for tackling it?

Avoid emotional leakage

Oh it can feel good to moan and rant and bitch about your situation. It's natural to want to talk about it and vent your frustrations. After all, being on the receiving end of a personal attack can feel traumatic in the extreme. But even if you are in a black pit of misery and at your lowest ebb, resist the urge to grumble.

You might get a little sympathy at first from your colleagues. But they don't really want to hear about it. There are certain rules that govern how we should behave at work. And bleating about how you are being singled out, marginalized, or harassed breaks one of them.

Think about when someone at work asks you "How are you?" When a busy colleague passes you in the corridor and asks you the question, what they want to hear is "Great" or "Fine thanks," rather than "My sciatica is playing up and my parents have just died in a fiery plane crash." Apart from your tight circle of close friends, most people simply don't want to hear too much about bad feelings.

Of course that doesn't mean that you can't feel emotions. Fear, anger, sadness, joy. They are all natural human reactions and I'd be more worried if you didn't feel any of them at all (as that would make you the textbook definition of a psychopath). And it's fine to tell people occasionally that you are afraid or angry, sad or happy. But know where to draw the line.

Do express your emotions. Don't waste your energies grumbling, whining and protesting to absolutely anyone who might be in the vicinity. Take control of the situation and deal with it instead.

Steer clear of official channels

Douglas wanted a better work–life balance. So he quit a high-flying private sector job to join a sleepy public sector organization. However, he quickly ran up against a rather nasty colleague, who regularly lost her temper and hurled verbal abuse at members of the team. She was universally acknowledged as a bully and Douglas refused to tolerate the situation – he started a grievance procedure against her.

Six months later, Douglas ended up leaving the organization. The bullying manager continues to work in the organization.

Unfortunately, official channels do not always deliver the right results and bringing HR and the management into the fray should be your last resort. Of course, in an ideal world, it should be your first resort. Official channels should be there to protect you. Your complaint should be investigated and your adversary would be removed and all would become right in the world.

But we don't live in an ideal world. We live in a reality in which organizations do what is best for the organization. Even if a particular HR manager may want to do the right thing by you, the situation may not turn out right for you. The HR manager usually reports to the HR director who reports to the big bosses of the organization. And so the big bosses will pressurize the HR director who will pressurize the HR manager to do what is best for the organization. So even though the HR manager may tell you that he or she is "on your side," can you trust them to act on it?

Even worse, complaining marks you out as a troublemaker, a stirrer, a pest. Someone who rocks the boat. Someone who should be quietly sidelined or removed from the organization rather than disturb the precious status quo.

So never forget that official decisions will always take into account what is best for the organization. In a dispute with a colleague, who has the greater value to the business? You or your adversary?

Douglas had failed to understand that his colleague had a long track record. For all her faults as a manager, the organization still needed her. They needed her too much for her rants and tyrannical leadership style to matter. They needed her more than they needed Douglas.

If you are under attack, your best bet is always to try to sort the situation out on your own through informal channels. Investigate the reasons for your adversary's attacks on you. Get a second opinion, and take action yourself. Always think twice before deciding to pursue official complaints.

Avoid resorting to underhand tactics

Ian, a consultant who responded in the Talentspace office politics survey, relates a tale of a chief executive needing to choose a managing director for a business unit. The two main candidates were set a task to see how well they worked together. Unfortunately, the two candidates spent so much time trying to make each other look stupid that they botched the task. The CEO ended up recruiting a new managing director externally, much to the chagrin of the internal candidates.

Antagonistic relationships usually lead to disaster for both parties. While it may be enjoyable to plot revenge on your adversary, it probably won't do your career any favors. Bringing about the downfall of your adversary might feel gratifying, but you could damage your own reputation so much that you end up shooting your career down in flames too.

What goes around comes around. Karma isn't just something that happens in the next life. Lie, wheedle, and cheat, and expect it to come back at you.

Remind yourself that you have set yourself certain career goals. And if a particular relationship needs to be salvaged, then do it for the sake of your career. Don't do it because it is the "right" thing to do. Do it because it helps you get to where you want to be. Grit your teeth, swallow your pride, and remind yourself that your goals are ultimately more important than the momentary satisfaction you may get from bringing about the downfall of an adversary.

Of course you might get away with using underhand tactics. But the likelihood is that you will get caught out. Unless you have made a regular habit of engaging in underhand tactics, you will find that it doesn't come easily to you. People will notice. And you will lose respect, trust, relationships. Being labeled as "political" or self-serving will set you back considerably in your ability to achieve your goals. So it's not that I necessarily have a moral issue with using underhand tactics – I'm just warning you that doing so is likely to get you into trouble. So don't do it. Ever.

Create a separate identity

Okay, I've spent enough time telling you what not to do. So what should you do?

The first step is to be very, very careful.

Jill, a graphics designer, felt that she was being bullied by her manager. Obviously she wasn't very happy about it but at the same time didn't really know what she could do about it. So she vented her frustrations in a small way by exchanging emails with a friend in another department, joking about the fiendish and excruciating tortures she secretly planned for her manager.

Unfortunately, she made the mistake of sending emails using her company-given email address. What happened next? You guessed it – her manager accessed her emails and presented Jill with transcripts of the exchanges. And while saying that you planned to poison your manager's coffee might seem funny between two colleagues, the HR department didn't take such a light-hearted view of it. Jill was fired and the other colleague received a black mark on his permanent employee record.

So the moral of the tale is to keep business and pleasure very separate. If you want to exchange email messages with a friend, trusted colleague, or confidant, make sure that it is with a personal email address that can't be invaded by your company's IT department. Hotmail, Yahoo, and their ilk provide free email accounts. Or if your company's firewall blocks offending sites, then make sure to wait until you get home before firing off email missives about the people you work with.

But it's not just email that can leave a trail. Make sure that you leave nothing incriminating behind. Even a scrap of paper tossed into a waste bin could be rescued by an adversary and used as evidence of your slanderous intent. So be careful. Be very careful.

Engage the enemy

It's probably the last thing you want to do, but the best way to tackle an adversary is to spend some quality one-on-one time with them. Bet that sounds like an enticing thought, doesn't it?

Whatever your adversary's motives, the best way to surface them is to have a face-to-face discussion. Rather than engaging in political maneuverings that could be complex and circuitous, get them alone in a quiet room. And try not to punch them in the face.

It takes courage to initiate a dialogue with someone who may have caused you anguish or misery for any number of weeks, months, or even years. But keep those career goals of yours in mind. If you have decided that this is a sufficiently important relationship to require repairing, then bite the bullet and do it.

Make an appointment to see your adversary. Drop innocently by their desk and ask if you could arrange to have a couple of moments of their time. If you can, take them away from prying eyes and ears. Suggest lunch in a sandwich bar or a drink in the pub. If all else fails, find an empty office with thick, thick walls.

A canny adversary might at try to wriggle out of a confrontation. Because they know that their tactics are likely to be exposed by discussion and scrutiny. But don't let them get away with it. They may cite work pressures and apologize that they can't make it. They might postpone time and again. But be patient. Don't blunder into a confrontation in front of others. Keep trying to nail them down. Ask them to suggest alternate times and dates. If they are busy next week and the week after, then how about the week after that? If they have a meeting at 9 am, couldn't they possibly arrive a half-hour earlier to have a chat with you?

Come on, you can do it. Do whatever it takes to get them alone with you in a room.

Embrace your dark side

But before you enter that room, embrace your dark side.

When I first heard the term "dark side" in a psychological context, I had images in my head of Darth Vader enticing Luke Skywalker to join him in ruling the galaxy.

But eminent psychologists have identified that we all have a dark side – or undesirable tendencies that may emerge when we are tired or bored or stressed or drunk or out of our comfort zone or otherwise let our guards down.

The theory goes that, under normal circumstances, we can control our darker tendencies and behave in a rational and effective manner. But when we aren't thinking clearly or when things aren't going well, our dark side might slip out.

For example, I know one manager who has a tendency to jump to conclusions. When she gets into uncomfortable situations, she tends to throw her hands in the air and make snap judgments that she has, on more than one occasion, later regretted. One of my ex-bosses had the opposite problem. He became incredibly indecisive under pressure, procrastinating and becoming unwilling to make a decision for fear of making the wrong one.

I know my dark side. If I'm honest with myself, I know that I have a tendency to let my

assertiveness turn into aggression and my irritation turn into anger. I blow up quite quickly. But
I also know people who behave in an almost
reverse fashion, withdrawing from confrontation
and going into a sulk.

Everyone has a dark side. You might see it
more often in some people than others. But
everyone has one – including you.

And it's important to understand your own
dark side. Because confronting an adversary is
tough. It's arguably one of the most difficult and
unnerving tasks you may ever take on at work. If
the discussion gets heated, you may find yourself
being unable to be as calm, cool and collected as
you would wish. And that's the precise moment
that your dark side might just emerge.

Discovering your dark side is the first step to
conquering it. Make it a priority to understand
yours.

Open up the can of worms

Turns out it's time to have words with your adversary. Click. The door closes behind you. Your palms feel a bit clammy and your breath seems to have caught in your throat. At last the two of you are alone. So what do you say?

Start by explaining that you sense an uneasiness between the two of you and simply want to sort it out. Even if you think that "uneasiness" is the mere tip of the iceberg, avoid using more evocative language. Avoid the temptation to scream and shout that they have been harassing and haranguing and terrorizing and intimidating you. Even if that's how you feel, choose your words carefully beforehand.

Then shut up. Don't give away all of the examples that you have readied as evidence. Stay quiet. Allow a silence to develop and hope for your adversary to crack.

Even if they don't say anything for a while, resist the temptation to speak up. Only when your adversary seems on the brink of leaving should you speak again. And then it should be only to reiterate that you sense an air of uneasiness between you. That the relationship isn't as good as it should be. Essentially repeat what you originally started off saying and no more.

Resist at all costs the urge to talk through the many examples you have readied. What your adversary says next will guide how you deal with them. By allowing a long, lingering silence to develop, you are providing just enough rope for your adversary to hang him or herself.

Present your case with care

Many adversaries will crack in the face of total silence. They will feel the need to justify themselves or offer up excuses of some sort.

But the small minority of ultra-cunning adversaries might simply reply that there's no problem. You're wasting your time. It's all in your head.

So continue by making it very clear that you are merely putting forwards your side of the story. Explain that this is your personal perspective and you are not claiming that all of it is correct. Even if you have a dozen colleagues to back you up, resist the urge to rub your adversary's nose in the issue.

Next, make it clear that you are not pointing the finger. Again, even if you secretly believe that your adversary is entirely to blame, at least pretend that you don't blame them. Remember that the goal here is not to be vindicated and be proved "right," but to sort out the situation and salvage the relationship and remove the person as an obstacle from your career path.

Then calmly and rationally describe the situation as you see it. Cite only one or two specific examples to back up what you are describing, but stop yourself from presenting your adversary with too many. Again, the point here is to illustrate with a few choice anecdotes rather than to condemn with a litany of sins.

To make it as unthreatening as possible, talk in the first person. Explain the situation from your personal perspective. Declaring "I get the impression that you are ignoring me" sounds less accusatory than "You are ignoring me." Remember that your adversary may not be aware of the impact that they are having on you – they may be useless rather than malicious.

At all costs keep a check on your dark side and avoid getting emotional or argumentative in your discussion. Speak for just a few minutes to begin with. And then give your opponent a chance to react.

Get at the truth

The truth is a messy business. People are so used to telling little white lies and saying what they think others want to hear at work. Honesty can sometimes feel like a rare commodity in the workplace.

So even when you tell an adversary your side of the situation and ask for them to comment, you may find they respond that nothing is wrong. It's all in your head – there's no problem.

But don't allow yourself to be fobbed off.

It's up to you as the more politically savvy person to push and persevere. Try different tactics to get the other person to open up. Because only when they open up and tell you what is bothering them or why they are behaving the way they do can you take steps to rectify the situation and repair the relationship.

Explain that the situation makes you incredibly uncomfortable. Show your vulnerable side and talk about how hurt you feel. Tell them about your sleepless nights and the misery you feel. This is the one occasion you can talk about how unhappy you may feel. Adversaries are usually ready for a confrontation, a shouting match – uninhibited unhappiness can often come as a surprise and be an unexpectedly disarming tactic. Say that you want to apologize if you are at fault in any way. Even if you are sure that you were not at fault, bite your lip and say it anyway – use it as a tactic to get your adversary to open up.

Do whatever it takes to get at the truth of the matter. Find out what the underlying issue or reason for the conflict is. So keep asking, pestering, imploring and persevering until you find out their issue with you. Because only then can you decide on the right course of action.

Contract with inadvertent adversaries

People make mistakes. And inadvertent adversaries are doing just that – making genuine mistakes. Okay, their mistakes may be causing you real grief, but the key here is to remember that it is unintentional. There is damage, but no deliberate malice.

An inadvertent adversary will generally be horrified by how you feel. When you tell them your side of the story and cite the evidence, you may see their jaws drop in shock at how they have unintentionally hurt you.

They may apologize and promise to take all sorts of actions to remedy the situation. But avoid the temptation of allowing yourself to feel smug. Even a hint of self-satisfaction at being proved right could be like pouring water on the sparks of your nascent relationship.

Instead reassure your adversary that no permanent harm was done. If you can bear it, suggest that some of the blame lay on your side too – perhaps for not having spoken up sooner or other reasons. Even if you don't believe that any of the blame ever lay on your side, it's still a good tactic to shoulder some of the burden and show good willing.

Then ask that the two of you agree on some ground rules for how you will behave towards each other. Go back through the situations in which you felt hurt. Retell the circumstances and ask your inadvertent adversary for suggestions on how to prevent them in the future.

Resist telling your adversary what you think needs to happen. Use open questions to get them to think. Encourage them to come up with suggestions and ideas so that they feel that it was their idea to behave in this new way. Get their input into a solution rather than ramming one down their throat.

If they keep leaving you out of invitations or important emails, decide on a system to help them remember. If they keep putting your requests for help at the bottom of their list of priorities, discuss a way to make sure it doesn't happen again. Create an implicit contract for how you will each behave towards each other.

With inadvertent adversaries, the hard work comes in broaching the subject. Once you have done that, you may find that they turn from adversary to ally in no time at all.

Reinforce frequently

Inadvertent adversaries are like young children or puppies. Rather than being a deliberate menace, they can't help but dribble and behave inappropriately. They are often as much of a danger to themselves as to others.

Your inadvertent adversary might be a bit incompetent or oblivious or both. But either way, just having a few simple words with them about how you feel may not always be enough to guarantee that they will mend their ways.

So train them up in the same way you might a dog or a young child. Just as you would reward a puppy with a pat on the head or a child an ice cream for good behavior, try to reinforce your inadvertent adversary's good new behaviors with profuse thanks and appreciation.

Surveys repeatedly show that the vast majority of employees feel that they don't receive enough thanks and recognition from the people around them. So make a special effort to thank them every time they remember to follow one of your ground rules.

Psychological research also shows that positive feedback works much more effectively than negative feedback to reinforce new behaviors. Tell someone off and they just resent you – they might do it again just to spite you. But praise someone and they feel good, they want to do it again and get more praise. So if you must remind them that they have forgotten to follow one of the new ground rules, tell them gently. Don't allow your irritation to get the better of you. Save your emotion for when they get something right and let yourself go over the top in showing your appreciation.

I'm sure you get the idea. Treat your inadvertent adversary like a naughty puppy or a misguided child and all will soon be right. Just don't tell them that's what you are doing.

Befriend insecure adversaries

How would you feel if you thought no one at work liked you? Or what if everyone at work actually hated you? You might feel left out, unhappy, defensive perhaps. Your behavior might change and slowly you'd slip into a spiral of incivility. After all, if they don't like you, why should you be nice to them? It's human nature to push back when you feel pushed away.

And that may be how insecure adversaries feel. The need for affection and a sense of belonging is a surprisingly powerful driver. An adversary may behave as one simply because of feeling rejected, left out, unwanted.

Now you may find it hard to believe that anyone could behave so badly towards you simply because they feel left out. But it happens, honestly. So one of the best tactics to deal with insecure adversaries is to make them feel included; try to offer yourself as a friend.

Of course it's probably the last thing you want to do. The notion of making friends with them probably fills you with abject horror. You feel upset, angry; you want to vent how you really feel. But that would be a big mistake. Huge.

Because this isn't about what you want to do, but what you must do. It isn't about making you feel better in the short term; it's about achieving your long-term career goals. The object of the exercise is to disarm your adversary. By doing what they least expect, by being politically savvy.

Befriending an insecure adversary works because most bullies genuinely crave a sense of belonging. They don't have the social skills to make friends. They lash out as a defense mechanism.

Don't get mad, don't get even. Someone famous once said "keep your friends close and your enemies closer" – well, this is my way of keeping enemies closer than a new pair of Lycra pants.

Fake it until you can make it

You may feel like a fraud and a fake for having to pretend to like your adversary. You probably loathe, detest, hate, and abhor the person. But don't think of pretending as a bad thing. Because a psychologist much older and wiser than me once told me that the key to learning any new skill or behavior is to "fake it until you can make it."

At first I didn't understand. But it actually makes perfect sense. If you are nervous about giving presentations, you don't tell your audience that you are nervous. You fake your confidence the first time. You fake it the next time. But the time after that you may find you start to feel a little more confident.

When I was in a situation of feeling intimidated and harassed by a colleague, I tried to fake it too. I made sure to stop by his desk every day to chat for a few minutes. I pretended that I was interested in what he had done the previous evening even though my stomach was churning. I even suggested going out for lunch. But then I found that I sometimes forgot I was pretending. And I did find his jokes funny and even enjoyed myself in his company at times. Eventually, we even developed a sort of grudging friendship. Most importantly perhaps, he was no longer obstructive and unhelpful. He was accommodating and attentive, supportive and cooperative.

The same goes for your adversary too. At first it will take every ounce of effort in your body to force a smile onto your face and pretend that you are interested in them or like them. Persevere with it. Persevere. Work hard and persevere some more. And you may surprise yourself and find that, as the days and weeks go by, you need to pretend less and less.

Make it your motto to bond with a bullying, insecure adversary. Not because it is the "fair" or "right" thing to do, but because it works to remove yet another obstacle in your career path.

Defer to revenge-motivated adversaries

It's that age-old quandary. Chicken or egg; egg or chicken. Which came first?

The problem with revenge-motivated adversaries is that they believe you started it all first. While you might find it difficult to believe, they genuinely see themselves as the injured party. And they see their behavior as a justifiable defense against whatever real or imagined act you committed.

It often happens that people get into protracted battles with each other without really remembering who started it all off first. But at the end of the day, it doesn't matter who started it. Have the courage to take the initiative. Put a stop to it all or the situation will never improve.

Once you have told them your side of the story, ask your adversary what their issues are. Ask if you have done anything wrong to upset them. Encourage them to tell you the matter.

You might be surprised by what they say. The initial slight or grievance may sound petty, trivial, insignificant. You probably won't believe they got so worked up over such a minor matter. But no matter. Whatever their issue, try to forgive even if you won't ever forget. Be the bigger person, apologize, and take the blame.

Of course you probably want to wring their neck rather than choke out an apology. But, as with insecure adversaries, remember that this is a political tactic on your part to neutralize your adversary. It's what you need to do rather than what you want to do. The words may stick in your throat, but fight to spit them out. Keep thinking about the career benefit – that you are taking the right steps to salvage an important relationship and limit the amount of career harm that your adversary may be inflicting on you.

So acknowledge their issue, listen to what they have to say and resist the temptation to defend yourself. Bite your tongue, dig your nails into your palm and do whatever it takes to nod sagely and shoulder the blame.

Because with revenge-motivated adversaries, you will find that simply talking about the issue openly and showing that you are willing to make amends is usually enough to defuse the situation and get the relationship on the mend. It clears the air, diffuses the tension. So get talking.

Collude with politically motivated adversaries

When a distribution business announced it was merging two of its business units, all hell broke loose. At least five of the senior managers were eligible for the top job and each started their political campaigns almost immediately – doubling their efforts to win over Bigwigs across the business while simultaneously encouraging rumors and highlighting faults and failings in each other. Eventually a clear winner emerged and he immediately appointed one of the other senior managers as deputy managing director.

As the dust settled, it became apparent that two of the candidates had agreed to collaborate rather than compete against each other. For one of the candidates, being number two in the enlarged business was better than being number none. Realizing that they could do so much more together than apart, they had teamed together to screw over the other candidates.

Possibly the most dangerous of all, politically motivated adversaries are not out to wreak havoc on your career because they enjoy it, but because they need to. Just like you, these rivals have career goals they want to achieve. They are motivated purely by ambition and the potential for personal gain. Perhaps they want a promotion, a pay rise, access to resources that only one person can have. And if they seem to be attacking you, they probably see you as yet another obstacle that needs to be removed for them to succeed.

But you might be able to broker a deal. Discuss your respective goals and check that you both even want the same prize. Sometimes an adversary might believe that you have the same goal when you don't. So clear the air, be explicit about what you want and encourage your adversary to do the same. Figure out not only their professional but also their personal agenda. Even if you both want the same prize, you might be able to negotiate a way to carve it up. Create your own little cartel. While someone usually has to lose out in such situations, try to find a way to ensure that it is not the two of you.

Contain when you can't collude

Often there can only be one winner. There's only one promotion available. Only one member of the team can be sent to that conference in the Caribbean. There's only one prize and the runner-up gets nothing.

If you can't collude with an adversary to reach some kind of compromise, then the last resort is containment. Damage control. Limit their impact on you.

Study their tactics and enlist the support of your allies. Double your efforts to build stronger relationships and accumulate more leverage with the Bigwigs who count.

If a competitor is trying to take the credit for your achievements, then alert your allies to their tactic. If your adversary is trying to enlarge their territory by pushing into yours, recruit your allies to help you push back. If your adversary is trying to misinform you or misdirect you, ask your allies to copy you in on all forms of communication even if it risks bombarding you with multiple copies of the same communiqués.

Cover your own back in any dealings with rivals too. Every time you have a conversation with them, use email to confirm actions, times, dates, places, and anything else that has been agreed. Don't let them get away with "forgetting" or blaming you for not following through on actions that you never agreed to take on in the first place. Take the precaution of sending yourself or even other interested colleagues copies if you think that there might be a risk of emails somehow "going astray."

Of course you could try your hand at the same kind of negative tactics. I've already mentioned I don't have a moral issue against being underhand. But you might get exposed and labeled "political." You could end up with a reputation as the kind of desperate, Machiavellian person who the Bigwigs will be loath to promote. Fight fire with fire and you could get burned.

Locate the emergency exits

Sometimes life just sucks. And there ain't nothing you can do about it.

I know of a recruitment agency in which the Chairman believes in speaking his mind. He speaks his mind to such an extent that he literally reduces members of the team to tears on pretty much a monthly basis. But there is little that anyone can do because he founded and owns the firm. For unhappy employees, the choice is only really either to put up with it or quit.

In a media business, there's a client director who has taken to drinking more than just the occasional glass of wine at lunchtimes. It makes her irritable and almost totally unable to manage her team effectively. But she still manages to pull in the big-spending clients so the business turns a blind eye to her behavior. For the hapless members of her team, their only choice is again to put up and shut up or look for another job.

Sometimes things just don't work out. Sometimes it's just the way it is. And in such unhappy times, you have two choices: take all the rubbish they throw at you and be miserable, or get out.

What would you do if things were to go horribly wrong? Do you network widely enough and know where the job opportunities are? Is your CV polished and ready to be sent off? It's a possibility that no one ever wants to consider. But then you're not just anybody. You're a politically savvy person who understands that we must always consider every possibility. Even those that we don't want to consider.

FINAL WORDS

And so we reach the end of our journey. I hope you go on to have a glorious and satisfying career.

But before we part company, here are my final thoughts for becoming organizationally effective and politically savvy. Consider it a summary of the key lessons to be learned:

- *Be a political animal.* People who "hate politics" or "don't do politics" inevitably get stuck in their careers. Because it's the people who do engage in politics who get ahead. The unwritten rules of politics are usually more important than what is written in your job description. Never forget that.
- *Build genuine relationships with people.* Strip away the fancy language, and political savvy is basically about people helping people they like. But the word "genuine" is key here. Be careful of trying to manipulate or screw over your colleagues. Word spreads quickly and you will lose trust quickly. Make sure that you are genuinely liked. It's as simple as that.
- *Remember that relationships don't just happen.* Becoming politically savvy is hard work. Relationships require perseverance, understanding, empathy, favors. Yes, some people may make their success look effortless, but don't be taken in. Behind the scenes they are working furiously hard at impressing and influencing.

- *Don't forget that not all people are created equal.* In an ideal world you might like to be nice to everyone. But in the real world, you have limited time, so prioritize. Focus on relationships with the few, key individuals who can help you to achieve your goals.

- *Understand that proactive politicking is twice as effective as reactive politicking.* Taking the time to assess the political territory around you and building relationships will stand you in better stead than blundering around and then trying to sort out unsatisfactory relationships afterwards. Observe, analyze, and build relationships slowly before you try to maneuver.

- *Keep thinking, re-evaluating, and planning.* Companies restructure and change direction. People rise and fall in prominence or disappear entirely. Their circumstances, motivations, and hot buttons may change too. So don't get complacent. Adapt your behavior and plans to match what goes on around you.

- *Don't just talk about it, do it.* Too many people whine about how "unfair" organizational life is. They complain about how they should have got the promotion or the pay rise or whatever else they failed to achieve. The people who succeed are the ones who keep quiet and figure out how to

get ahead. Take control, take responsibility.
Make things happen.

It's treacherous out there. But with patience and
planning, anyone can become sufficiently politically savvy to succeed. I would wish you good luck.
But as you should know by now, luck has little to
do with success. Go create your own success.

ALSO BY ROB YEUNG

The Rules of EQ

In today's demanding business world, it takes more than brains and hard work to get along. Those who succeed have another quality in common: emotional intelligence.

In this readable introduction, Yeung explains how to up your "EQ" – your emotional intelligence quotient – and to use it to get ahead at work. He encourages you to get to know, and control, your own emotions, to become self-directed, resilient and success-oriented. Learn how to overcome setbacks and achieve success.

The tips in this book can set you on the road to greater happiness and greater success. A higher EQ is yours for the taking.

Praise for *The Rules of EQ*:

"Savvy and timely, ... a valuable tool in the arsenal of the effective business person." Independent Publishers Group

"Intelligent writing broken down into easy-to-read chapters." Amazon customer review

"The book has been quoted in publications ranging from *Men's Health* and *Psychologies* to *Accountancy* and *The Guardian*." Talentspace News3

ISBN 981 261 812 0 (Asia & ANZ)
ISBN 1-904879-37-3 (Rest of world)
UK £9.99 / USA $17.95 / CAN $24.95

ALSO BY ROB YEUNG

The Rules of Networking

Networking – probably the single most essential skill required of all bright professionals hoping to progress in their chosen career path. Yet no ever teaches it to you. Help is finally at hand: this book is a snappy, step-by-step guide, which is designed to steer you safely through the unpredictable battlefield of modern working life.

This easy-to-follow guide is packed with hints and tips: advice on how to become the center of attention, how to ensure your fellow networkers pocket, rather than bin your business card, and how to build relationships in which people will be falling over themselves to help you achieve your goals.

Praise for *The Rules of Networking*:

"The books in this series are designed to be read in only a couple of hours and are perfect educational reading for business trips. ... The lessons are succinct and to the point." Independent Publishers Group

"This book is going to help you to find the right people." Amazon customer review

"Networking has become one of the key skills for virtually anyone who wants to get ahead in their jobs. ... Savvy and practical advice on networking that will make a genuine difference to your career." Amazon

ISBN 981 261 813 9 (Asia & ANZ)
ISBN 1-904879-38-1 (Rest of world)
UK £9.99 / USA $17.95 / CAN $24.95

ALSO BY ROB YEUNG

The Rules of Job Hunting

Job hunting used to be a simple process: send off a CV, go for an interview and, if you were the best candidate, get offered the job. Now the procedure is more complex.

Don't worry, help is at hand! In a book filled with tips and insider advice on understanding the product, creating a winning CV, opening up opportunities, being unforgettable at interviews, and signing on the dotted line, Rob Yeung explains exactly how to succeed and land yourself a great job.

The Rules of Job Hunting is short and full of practical, pithy advice in bite-sized chunks, and a book you must buy if you are to find the perfect job!

Praise for *The Rules of Job Hunting*

"*The Rules of Job Hunting* is the best book of its kind I have read in 20 years in this field. Packed with practical advice, new ideas, and essential insights, it is a 'must read' for all who are seeking that elusive next move." Richard Chiumento, Chief Executive Officer, Rialto, human resources consultancy

"*The Rules of Job Hunting* covers the spectrum of job-hunting activities from networking and dealing with headhunters to interviewing and negotiating contracts. It's essential reading for job hunters at any level." Joe Slavin, Chief Executive Officer of top job-hunting website fish4jobs.co.uk

ISBN-13 978-1-904879-86-2
ISBN-10 1-904879-86-1
UK £9.99 / USA $17.95 / CAN $24.95